C-531   CAREER EXAMINATION SERIES

This is your
PASSBOOK for...

Notary Public

Test Preparation Study Guide
Questions & Answers

NATIONAL LEARNING CORPORATION®

COPYRIGHT NOTICE

This book is SOLELY intended for, is sold ONLY to, and its use is RESTRICTED to individual, bona fide applicants or candidates who qualify by virtue of having seriously filed applications for appropriate license, certificate, professional and/or promotional advancement, higher school matriculation, scholarship, or other legitimate requirements of education and/or governmental authorities.

This book is NOT intended for use, class instruction, tutoring, training, duplication, copying, reprinting, excerption, or adaptation, etc., by:

1) Other publishers
2) Proprietors and/or Instructors of "Coaching" and/or Preparatory Courses
3) Personnel and/or Training Divisions of commercial, industrial, and governmental organizations
4) Schools, colleges, or universities and/or their departments and staffs, including teachers and other personnel
5) Testing Agencies or Bureaus
6) Study groups which seek by the purchase of a single volume to copy and/or duplicate and/or adapt this material for use by the group as a whole without having purchased individual volumes for each of the members of the group
7) Et al.

Such persons would be in violation of appropriate Federal and State statutes.

PROVISION OF LICENSING AGREEMENTS – Recognized educational, commercial, industrial, and governmental institutions and organizations, and others legitimately engaged in educational pursuits, including training, testing, and measurement activities, may address request for a licensing agreement to the copyright owners, who will determine whether, and under what conditions, including fees and charges, the materials in this book may be used them. In other words, a licensing facility exists for the legitimate use of the material in this book on other than an individual basis. However, it is asseverated and affirmed here that the material in this book CANNOT be used without the receipt of the express permission of such a licensing agreement from the Publishers. Inquiries re licensing should be addressed to the company, attention rights and permissions department.

All rights reserved, including the right of reproduction in whole or in part, in any form or by any means, electronic or mechanical, including photocopying, recording, or by any information storage and retrieval system, without permission in writing from the Publisher.

Copyright © 2024 by
National Learning Corporation

212 Michael Drive, Syosset, NY 11791
(516) 921-8888 • www.passbooks.com
E-mail: info@passbooks.com

PUBLISHED IN THE UNITED STATES OF AMERICA

PASSBOOK® SERIES

THE *PASSBOOK® SERIES* has been created to prepare applicants and candidates for the ultimate academic battlefield – the examination room.

At some time in our lives, each and every one of us may be required to take an examination – for validation, matriculation, admission, qualification, registration, certification, or licensure.

Based on the assumption that every applicant or candidate has met the basic formal educational standards, has taken the required number of courses, and read the necessary texts, the *PASSBOOK® SERIES* furnishes the one special preparation which may assure passing with confidence, instead of failing with insecurity. Examination questions – together with answers – are furnished as the basic vehicle for study so that the mysteries of the examination and its compounding difficulties may be eliminated or diminished by a sure method.

This book is meant to help you pass your examination provided that you qualify and are serious in your objective.

The entire field is reviewed through the huge store of content information which is succinctly presented through a provocative and challenging approach – the question-and-answer method.

A climate of success is established by furnishing the correct answers at the end of each test.

You soon learn to recognize types of questions, forms of questions, and patterns of questioning. You may even begin to anticipate expected outcomes.

You perceive that many questions are repeated or adapted so that you can gain acute insights, which may enable you to score many sure points.

You learn how to confront new questions, or types of questions, and to attack them confidently and work out the correct answers.

You note objectives and emphases, and recognize pitfalls and dangers, so that you may make positive educational adjustments.

Moreover, you are kept fully informed in relation to new concepts, methods, practices, and directions in the field.

You discover that you are actually taking the examination all the time: you are preparing for the examination by "taking" an examination, not by reading extraneous and/or supererogatory textbooks.

In short, this PASSBOOK®, used directedly, should be an important factor in helping you to pass your test.

NOTARY PUBLIC

DUTIES

A notary is a public officer whose main functions are to administer oaths and affirmations, take affidavits and statutory declarations, witness and authenticate the execution of certain classes of documents, take acknowledgments of deeds and other conveyances, protest notes and bills of exchange, provide notice of foreign drafts, prepare marine or ship's protests in cases of damage, provide exemplifications and notarial copies, and perform certain other official acts depending on the jurisdiction. While all states allow their notaries to perform oaths/affirmations and acknowledgments, whether or not a notary may perform any other duties varies by state, depending on each state's unique notary laws. Notaries are expected to know and honor what their state laws allow them to do.

SCOPE OF THE EXAMINATION

The written test will cover knowledge, skills, and /or abilities in such areas as:
1. Notarial duties, principles, practices, rules and regulations;
2. Legal terminology; and
3. Documents and forms.

Notary Public License Law

Introduction

Notary publics are commissioned by the Secretary of State. An applicant for a notary public commission must submit to the Division of Licensing Services an original application and $60 fee. The application includes an oath of office, which must be sworn and notarized. In addition to the application form and fee, the applicant must submit a "pass slip" showing that s/he has taken and passed the notary public examination. Examinations are regularly scheduled throughout the state. An individual admitted to practice in NYS as an attorney, may be appointed a notary public without an examination. The term of commission is 4 years.

Notary publics are commissioned in their counties of residence. After receiving and approving an applicant for a notary public commission, the Secretary of State forwards the commission, the original oath of office and the signature of the notary public to the appropriate county clerk. The county clerk maintains a record of the commission and signature. The public may then access this record and verify the "official" signature of the notary at the county clerk's office.

Upon request, county clerks will authenticate the signature of the notary on a document and will attest to the notary's authority to sign. This is normally obtained when the documents will be used outside the State. Notaries who expect to sign documents regularly in counties other than that of their residence may elect to file a certificate of official character with other New York State county clerks.

Out-of-State Residents. Attorneys, residing out of State, who are admitted to practice in the State and who maintain a law office within the State are deemed to be residents of the county where the office is maintained. Nonresidents other than attorneys who have offices or places of business in New York State may also become notaries. The oath of office and signature of the notary must be filed in the office of the county clerk of the county in which the office or place of business is located.

Notary Public License Law

Section		
	Professional conduct	
		APPOINTMENT AND QUALIFICATIONS EXECUTIVE LAW
130	Appointment of notaries public	

131	Procedure of appointment; fees and commissions
132	Certificates of official character of notaries public
133	Certification of notarial signatures
140	Executive Law (14) and (15)
3-200 and 3-400	Election Law

PUBLIC OFFICERS LAW

3	Qualifications for holding office

COUNTY LAW

534	County clerk; appointment of notaries public

MISCELLANEOUS

Member of legislature

Sheriffs

Notary public--disqualifications

POWERS AND DUTIES EXECUTIVE LAW

134	Signature and seal of county clerk
135	Powers and duties; in general; of notaries public who are attorneys at law
135-a	Notary public or commissioner of deeds; acting without appointment; fraud in office
136	Notarial fees
137	Statement as to authority of notaries public
138	Powers of notaries public or other officers who are stockholders, directors, officers or employees of a corporation
142-a	Validity of facts of notaries public and commissioners of deeds notwithstanding certain defects

REAL PROPERTY LAW

290	Definitions; effect of article
298	Acknowledgments and proofs within the state
302	Acknowledgments and proofs by married women
303	Requisites of acknowledgments
304	Proof by subscribing witness
306	Certificate of acknowledgment or proof
309-a	Uniform forms of certificates of acknowledgment or proof within this state
309-b	Uniform forms of certificates of acknowledgment or proof without this state
330	Officers guilty of malfeasance liable for damages
333	When conveyances of real property not to be recorded

SPECIAL NOTE

335	Banking Law
3113	Rule—Civil Practice Law and Rules
11	Domestic Relations Law
10	Public Officers Law

RESTRICTIONS AND VIOLATIONS JUDICIARY LAW

484	None but attorneys to practice in the state
485	Violation of certain preceding sections a misdemeanor
750	Power of courts to punish for criminal contempts
	Illegal practice of law by notary public
	Wills

PUBLIC OFFICERS LAW

67	Fees of public officers
69	Fee for administering certain official oaths prohibited

EXECUTIVE LAW

Misconduct by a notary and removal from office

PENAL LAW

70.00	Sentence of imprisonment for felony
70.15	Sentences of imprisonment for misdemeanors and violation
170.10	Forgery in the second degree
175.40	Issuing a false certificate
195.00	Official misconduct
	Notary must officiate on request
	Perjury

DEFINITIONS AND GENERAL TERMS

Use of the office of notary in other than the specific, step-by-step procedure required is viewed as a serious offense by the Secretary of State. The practice of taking acknowledgments and affidavits over the telephone, or otherwise, without the actual, personal appearance of the individual making the acknowledgment or affidavit before the officiating notary, is illegal.

The attention of all notaries public is called to the following judicial declarations concerning such misconduct:

"The court again wishes to express its condemnation of the acts of notaries taking acknowledgments or affidavits without the presence of the party whose acknowledgment is taken for the affiant, and that it will treat serious professional misconduct the act of any notary thus violating his official duty." (*Matter of Napolis*, 169 App. Div. 469, 472.)

"Upon the faith of these acknowledgments rests the title of real property, and the only security to such titles is the fidelity with which notaries and commissioners of deeds perform their duty in requiring the appearance of parties to such instruments before them and always refusing to execute a certificate unless the parties are actually known to them or the identity of the parties executing the instruments is satisfactorily proved." (*Matter of Gottheim*, 153 App. Div. 779, 782.)

Equally unacceptable to the Secretary of State is slipshod administration of oaths. **The simplest form in which an oath may be lawfully administered is:**

"Do you solemnly swear that the contents of this affidavit subscribed by you is correct and true?" (*Bookman v. City of New York*, 200 N.Y. 53, 56.)

Alternatively, the following affirmation may be used for persons who conscientiously decline taking an oath. This affirmation is legally equivalent to an oath and is just as binding:

"Do you solemnly, sincerely and truly declare and affirm that the statements made by you are true and correct?"

Whatever the form adopted, it must be in the presence of an officer authorized to administer it, and it must be an unequivocal and present act by which the affiant consciously takes upon himself the obligation of an oath. (Idem, citing People ex rel. *Kenyan v. Sutherland*, 81 N.Y. 1; *O'Reilly v. People*, 86 N.Y. 154, 158, 161.)

Unless a lawyer, the notary public may not engage directly or indirectly in the practice of law. Listed below are some of the activities involving the practice of law which are prohibited, and which subject the notary public to removal from office by the Secretary of State, and possible imprisonment, fine or both. A notary:

1. May not give advice on the law. The notary may not draw any kind of legal papers, such as wills, deeds, bills of sale, mortgages, chattel mortgages, contracts, leases, offers, options, incorporation papers, releases, mechanics liens, power of attorney, complaints and all legal pleadings, papers in summary proceedings to evict a tenant, or in bankruptcy, affidavits, or any papers which our courts have said are legal documents or papers.

2. May not ask for and get legal business to send to a lawyer or lawyers with whom he has any business connection or from whom he receives any money or other consideration for sending the business.

3. May not divide or agree to divide his fees with a lawyer, or accept any part of a lawyer's fee on any legal business.

4. May not advertise in, or circulate in any manner, any paper or advertisement, or say to anyone that he has any powers or rights not given to the notary by the laws under which the notary was appointed.

A notary public is cautioned not to execute an acknowledgment of the execution of a will. Such acknowledgment cannot be deemed equivalent to an attestation clause accompanying a will. *(See definition of Attestation Clause)*

Appointment and Qualifications

Index

Law	Sec	Subject
Executive Law	130	Appointment of Notaries Public
Executive Law	131	Procedure of Appointment; Fees
Executive Law	132	Certificates of Official Character
Executive Law	133	Certification of Notarial Signatures

Executive Law	140	Commissioner of Deeds, NYC
Election Law	3-200 3-400	Commissioner of Elections
Public Officers Law	3	Qualifications for Holding Office
County Law	534	County Clerk; Appointment of Notaries
NYS Constitution	Art. II Sec.7	Member of Legislature
NYSConstitution	Art. XIII Sec.l3a	Sheriffs
Miscellaneous		Disqualifications

Executive Law

§130. Appointment of notaries public.

The Secretary of State may appoint and commission as many notaries public for the State of New York as in his or her judgment may be deemed best, whose jurisdiction shall be co-extensive with the boundaries of the state. The appointment of a notary public shall be for a term of 4 years. An application for an appointment as notary public shall be in form and set forth such matters as the Secretary of State shall prescribe. Every person appointed as notary public must, at the time of his or her appointment, be a citizen of the United States and either a resident of the State of New York or have an office or place of business in New York State. A notary public who is a resident of the State and who moves out of the state but still maintains a place of business or an office in New York State does not vacate his or her office as a notary public. A notary public who is a nonresident and who ceases to have an office or place of business in this state, vacates his or her office as a notary public. A notary public who is a resident of New York State and moves out of the state and who does not retain an office or place of business in this State shall vacate his or her office as a notary public. A non-resident who accepts the office of notary public in this State thereby appoints the Secretary of State as the person upon whom process can be served on his or her behalf. Before issuing to any applicant a commission as notary public, unless he or she be an attorney and counselor at law duly admitted to practice in this state or a court clerk of the Unified Court System who has been appointed to such position after taking a Civil Service promotional examination in the court clerk series of titles, the Secretary of State shall satisfy himself or herself that the applicant is of good moral character, has the equivalent of a common school education and is familiar with the duties and responsibilities of a notary public; provided, however, that where a notary public applies, before the expiration of his or her term, for reappointment with the county clerk or where a person whose term as notary public shall have expired applies within 6 months thereafter for reappointment as a notary public with the county clerk, such qualifying requirements may be waived by the Secretary of State, and further, where an application for reappointment is filed with the county clerk after the expiration of the aforementioned renewal period by a person who failed or was unable to re-apply by reason of his or her induction or enlistment in the armed forces of the United States, such qualifying requirements may also be waived by the Secretary of State, provided such application for reappointment is made within a period of 1 year after the military discharge of the applicant under conditions other than dishonorable. In any case, the appointment or reappointment of any applicant is in the discretion of the Secretary of State. The Secretary of State may suspend or remove from office, for misconduct, any notary public appointed by him or her but no such removal shall be made unless the person who is sought to be removed shall have been served with a copy of the charges against him or her and have an opportunity of being heard. No person shall be appointed as a notary public under this article who has been convicted, in this State or any other state or territory, of a felony or any of the following offenses, to wit:

(a) illegally using, carrying or possessing a pistol or other dangerous weapon;
(b) making or possessing burglar's instruments;
(c) buying or receiving or criminally possessing stolen property;
(d) unlawful entry of a building;
(e) aiding escape from prison;
(f) unlawfully possessing or distributing habit forming narcotic drugs;
(g) violating §§270, 270-a, 270-b, 270-c, 271, 275, 276, 550, 551, 551-a and subdivisions 6, 8, 10 or 11 of § 722 of the former Penal Law as in force and effect immediately prior to September 1, 1967, or violating §§ 165.25,165.30, subdivision 1 of § 240.30, subdivision 3 of § 240.35 of the Penal Law, or violating §§478, 479, 480, 481, 484, 489 and 491 of the Judiciary Law; or
(h) vagrancy or prostitution, and who has not subsequent to such conviction received an executive pardon therefor or a certificate of good conduct from the parole board to remove the disability under this section because of such conviction. A person regularly admitted to practice as an attorney and counselor in the courts of record of this state, whose office for the practice of law is within the State, may be appointed a notary public and retain his office as such notary public although he resides in or removes to an adjoining state. For the purpose of this and the following sections of this article such person shall be deemed a resident of the county where he maintains such office.

§131. Procedure of appointment; fees and commissions.

1. Applicants for a notary public commission shall submit to the Secretary of State with their application the oath of office, duly executed before any person authorized to administer an oath, together with their signature.

2. Upon being satisfied of the competency and good character of applicants for appointment as notaries public, the Secretary of State shall issue a commission to such persons; and the official signature of the applicants and the oath of office filed with such applications shall take effect.

3. The Secretary of State shall receive a non-refundable application fee of $60 from applicants for appointment, which fee shall be submitted together with the application. No further fee shall be paid for the issuance of the commission.

4. A notary public identification card indicating the appointee's name, address, county and commission term shall be transmitted to the appointee.

5. The commission, duly dated, and a certified copy or the original of the oath of office and the official signature, and $20 apportioned from the application fee shall be transmitted by the Secretary of State to the county clerk in which the appointee resides by the 10th day of the following month.

6. The county clerk shall make a proper index of commissions and official signatures transmitted to that office by the Secretary of State pursuant to the provisions of this section.

7. Applicants for reappointment of a notary public commission shall submit to the county clerk with their application the oath of office, duly executed before any person authorized to administer an oath, together with their signature.

8. Upon being satisfied of the completeness of the application for reappointment, the county clerk shall issue a commission to such persons; and the official signature of the applicants and the oath of office filed with such applications shall take effect.

9. The county clerk shall receive a non-refundable application fee of $60 from each applicant for reappointment, which fee shall be submitted together with the application. No further fee shall be paid for the issuance of the commission.

10. The commission, duly dated, and a certified or original copy of the application, and $40 apportioned from the application fee plus interest as may be required by statute shall be transmitted by the county clerk to the Secretary of State by the 10th day of the following month.

11. The Secretary of State shall make a proper record of commissions transmitted to that office by the county clerk pursuant to the provisions of this section.

12. Except for changes made in an application for reappointment, the Secretary of State shall receive a non-refundable fee of $10 for changing the name or address of a notary public.

13. The Secretary of State may issue a duplicate identification card to a notary public for one lost, destroyed or damaged upon application therefor on a form prescribed by the Secretary of State and upon payment of a non-refundable fee of $10. Each such duplicate identification card shall have the word "duplicate" stamped across the face thereof, and shall bear the same number as the one it replaces.

§132. Certificates of official character of notaries public.

The Secretary of State or the county clerk of the county in which the commission of a notary public is filed may certify to the official character of such notary public and any notary public may file his autograph signature and a certificate of official character in the office of any county clerk of any county in the State and in any register's office in any county having a register and thereafter such county clerk may certify as to the official character of such notary public. The Secretary of State shall collect for each certificate of official character issued by him the sum of $10. The county clerk and register of any county with whom a certificate of official character has been filed shall collect for filing the same the sum of $10. For each certificate of official character issued, with seal attached, by any county clerk, the sum of $5 shall be collected by him.

§133. Certification of notarial signatures.

The county clerk of a county in whose office any notary public has qualified or has filed his autograph signature and a certificate of his official character, shall, when so requested and upon payment of a fee of $3 affix to any certificate of proof or acknowledgment or oath signed by such notary anywhere in the State of New York, a certificate under his hand and seal, stating that a commission or a certificate of his official character with his autograph signature has been filed in his office, and that he was at the time of taking such proof or acknowledgment or oath duly authorized to take the same; that he is well acquainted with the handwriting of such notary public or has compared the signature on the certificate of proof or acknowledgment or oath with the autograph signature deposited in his office by such notary public and believes that the signature is genuine. An instrument with such certificate of authentication of the county clerk affixed thereto shall be entitled to be read in evidence or to be recorded in any of the counties of this State in respect to which a certificate of a county clerk may be necessary for either purpose.

§140. Executive Law.

14. No person who has been removed from office as a commissioner of deeds for the City of New York, as hereinbefore provided, shall thereafter be eligible again to be appointed as such commissioner nor, shall he be eligible thereafter to appoint to the office of notary public.

15. Any person who has been removed from office as aforesaid, who shall, after knowledge of such removal, sign or execute any instrument as a commissioner of deeds or notary public shall be deemed guilty of a misdemeanor.

§§3-200 and 3-400. Election Law.
A commissioner of elections or inspector of elections is eligible for the office of notary public.

§3. Public Officers Law.
No person is eligible for the office of notary public who has been convicted of a violation of the selective draft act of the U.S. enacted May 18, 1917, or the acts amendatory or supplemental thereto, or of the federal selective training and service act of 1940 or the acts amendatory thereof or supplemental thereto.

§534. County Law.
Each county clerk shall designate from among the members of his or her staff at least one notary public to be available to notarize documents for the public in each county clerk's office during normal business hours free of charge. Each individual appointed by the county clerk to be a notary public pursuant to this section shall be exempt from the examination fee and application fee required by §131 of the Executive Law.

Miscellaneous

Member of legislature.
"If a member of the legislature be *** appointed to any office, civil *** under the government *** the State of New York *** his or her acceptance thereof shall vacate his or her seat in the legislature, providing, however, that a member of the legislature may be appointed *** to any office in which he or she shall receive no compensation." (§7 of Article III of the Constitution of the State of New York.) A member of the legislature may be appointed a notary public in view of transfer of power of such appointment from the governor and senate to the Secretary of State. (1927, Op. Atty. Gen. 97.)

Sheriffs.
*** Sheriffs shall hold no other office. *** (§13(a) of Article XIII of the Constitution of the State of New York.)

Notary public—disqualifications.
Though a person may be eligible to hold the office of notary the person may be disqualified to act in certain cases by reason of having an interest in the case. To state the rule broadly: if the notary is a party to or directly and pecuniarily interested in the transaction, the person is not capable of acting in that case. For example, a notary who is a grantee or mortgagee in a conveyance or mortgage is disqualified to take the acknowledgment of the grantor or mortgagor; likewise a notary who is a trustee in a deed of trust; and, of course, a notary who is the grantor could not take his own acknowledgment. A notary beneficially interested in the conveyance by way of being secured thereby is not competent to take the acknowledgment of the instrument. In New York the courts have held an acknowledgment taken by a person financially or beneficially interested in a party to conveyance or instrument of which it is a part to be a nullity; and that the acknowledgment of an assignment of a mortgage before one of the assignees is a nullity; and that an acknowledgment by one of the incorporators of the other incorporators who signed a certificate was of no legal effect.

Powers and Duties

Index

Law	Sec	Subject
Executive Law	134	Signature and Seal of County Clerk
Executive Law	135	Powers and Duties
Executive Law	135a	Acting Without Appointment, Fraud in Office
Executive Law	136	Notarial Fees
Executive Law	137	Statement as to authority
Executive Law	138	Powers of Notaries - Corporations
Executive Law	142-a	Validity of facts
Real Property Law	290	Definitions
Real Property Law	298	Acknowledgments and Proofs within the State
Real Property Law	302	Acknowledgments and Proofs By Married Women
Real Property Law	303	Requisites of Acknowledgments
Real Property Law	304	Proof by Subscribing Wit ness
Real Property Law	306	Certificate of Acknowledg ment or Proof
Real Property Law	309	Acknowledgment by Corporation
Real Property Law	330	Officers Guilty of Malfeasance
Real Property Law	333	When Conveyances Not to Be Recorded
Banking Law	335	Unpaid Rental of Safe De posit Box
Civil Practice Law and Rules	3113	Taking of Deposition by Notary
Domestic Relation	S11	No Authority to Solemnize Marriage
Public Officers	10	Administering Oath of Public Officer

Executive Law

§134. Signature and seal of county clerk.

The signature and seal of a county clerk, upon a certificate of official character of a notary public or the signature of a county clerk upon a certificate of authentication of the signature and acts of a notary public or commissioner of deeds, may be a facsimile, printed, stamped, photographed or engraved thereon.

§135. Powers and duties; in general; of notaries public who are attorneys at law.

Every notary public duly qualified is hereby authorized and empowered within and throughout the State to administer oaths and affirmations, to take affidavits and depositions, to receive and certify acknowledgments or proof of deeds, mortgages and powers of attorney and other instruments in writing; to demand acceptance or payment of foreign and inland bills of exchange, promissory notes and obligations in writing, and to protest the same for non-acceptance or non-payment, as the case may require, and, for use in another jurisdiction, to exercise such other powers and duties as by the laws of nations and according to commercial usage, or by the laws of any other government or country may be exercised and performed by notaries public, provided that when exercising such powers he shall set forth the name of such other jurisdiction.

A notary public who is an attorney at law regularly admitted to practice in this State may, in his discretion, administer an oath or affirmation to or take the affidavit or acknowledgment of his client in respect of any matter, claim, action or proceeding.

For any misconduct by a notary public in the performance of any of his powers such notary public shall be liable to the parties injured for all damages sustained by them. A notary public shall not, directly or indirectly, demand or receive for the protest for the non-payment of any note, or for the non-acceptance or non-payment of any bill of exchange, check or draft and giving the requisite notices and certificates of such protest, including his notarial seal, if affixed thereto, any greater fee or reward than 75 cents for such protest, and 10 cents for each notice, not exceeding five, on any bill or note. Every notary public having a seal shall, except as otherwise provided, and when requested, affix his seal to such protest free of expense.

§135-a. Notary public or commissioner of deeds; acting without appointment; fraud in office.

1. Any person who holds himself out to the public as being entitled to act as a notary public or commissioner of deeds, or who assumes, uses or advertises the title of notary public or commissioner of deeds, or equivalent terms in any language, in such a manner as to convey the impression that he is a notary public or commissioner of deeds without having first been appointed as notary public or commissioner of deeds, or

2. A notary public or commissioner of deeds, who in the exercise of the powers, or in the performance of the duties of such office shall practice any fraud or deceit, the punishment for which is not otherwise provided for by this act, shall be guilty of a misdemeanor.

§136. Notarial fees.

A notary public shall be entitled to the following fees:

1. For administering an oath or affirmation, and certifying the same when required, except where another fee is specifically prescribed by statute, $2.

2. For taking and certifying the acknowledgment or proof of execution of a written instrument, by one person, $2, and by each additional person, $2, for swearing such witness thereto, $2.

§137. Statement as to authority of notaries public.

In exercising his powers pursuant to this article, a notary public, in addition to the venue of his act and his signature, shall print, typewrite, or stamp beneath his signature in black ink, his name, the words "Notary Public State of New York," the name of the county in which he originally qualified, and the date upon which his commission expires and, in addition, wherever required, a notary public shall also include the name of any county in which his certificate of official character is filed, using the words "Certificate filed....................County." A notary public who is duly licensed as an attorney and counselor at law in this State may in his discretion, substitute the words "Attorney and Counselor at Law" for the words "Notary Public." A notary public who has qualified or who has filed a certificate of official character in the office of the clerk in a county or counties within the City of New York must also affix to each instrument his official number or numbers in black ink, as given to him by the clerk or clerks of such county or counties at the time such notary qualified in such county or counties and, if the instrument is to be recorded in an office of the register of the City of New York in any county within such city and the notary has been given a number or numbers by such register or his predecessors in any county or counties, when his autographed signature and certificate are filed in such office or offices pursuant to this chapter, he shall also affix such number or numbers. No official act of such notary public shall be held invalid on account of the failure to comply with these provisions. If any notary public shall wilfully fail to comply with any of the provisions of this section, he shall be subject to disciplinary action by the secretary of state. In all the courts within this State the certificate of a notary public, over his signature, shall be received as presumptive evidence of the facts contained in such certificate; provided, that any person interested as a party to a suit may contradict, by other evidence, the certificate of a notary public.

§138. Powers of notaries public or other officers who are stockholders, directors, officers or employees of a corporation.

A notary public, justice of the supreme court, a judge, clerk, deputy clerk, or special deputy clerk of a court, an official examiner of title, or the mayor or recorder of a city, a justice of the peace, surrogate, special surrogate, special county judge, or commissioner of deeds, who is a stockholder, director, officer or employee of a corporation may take the acknowledgment or proof of any party to a written instrument executed to or by such corporation, or administer an oath of any other stockholder, director, officer, employee or agent of such corporation, and such notary public may protest for non- acceptance or nonpayment, bills of exchange, drafts, checks, notes and other negotiable instruments owned or held for collection by such corporation; but none of the officers above named shall take the acknowledgment or proof of a written instrument by or to a corporation of which he is a stockholder, director, officer or employee, if such officer taking such acknowledgment or proof to be a party executing such instrument, either individually or as representative of such corporation, nor shall a notary public protest any negotiable instruments owned or held for collection by such corporation, if such notary public be individually a party to such instrument, or have a financial interest in the subject of same. All such acknowledgments or proofs of deeds, mortgages or other written instruments, relating to real property heretofore taken before any of the officers aforesaid are confirmed. This act shall not affect any action or legal proceeding now pending.

§142-a. Validity of acts of notaries public and commissioners of deeds notwithstanding certain defects.

1. Except as provided in subdivision three of this section, the official certificates and other acts heretofore or hereafter made or performed of notaries public and commissioners of deeds heretofore or hereafter and prior to the time of their acts appointed or commissioned as such shall not be deemed invalid, impaired or in any manner defective, so far as they may be affected, impaired or questioned by reason of defects described in subdivision two of this section.

2. This section shall apply to the following defects:

(a) ineligibility of the notary public or commissioner of deeds to be appointed or commissioned as such;

(b) misnomer or misspelling of name or other error made in his appointment or commission;

(c) omission of the notary public or commissioner of deeds to take or file his official oath or otherwise qualify;

(d) expiration of his term, commission or appointment;

(e) vacating of his office by change of his residence, by acceptance of another public office, or by other action on his part;

(f) the fact that the action was taken outside the jurisdiction where the notary public or commissioner of deeds was authorized to act.

3. No person shall be entitled to assert the effect of this section to overcome a defect described in subdivision two if he knew of the defect or if the defect was apparent on the face of the certificate of the notary public or commissioner of deeds; provided however, that this subdivi-

sion shall not apply after the expiration of six months from the date of the act of the notary public or commissioner of deeds.

4. After the expiration of six months from the date of the official certificate or other act of the commissioner of deeds, subdivision one of this section shall be applicable to a defect consisting in omission of the certificate of a commissioner of deeds to state the date on which and the place in which an act was done, or consisting of an error in such statement.

5. This section does not relieve any notary public or commissioner of deeds from criminal liability imposed by reason of his act, or enlarge the actual authority of any such officer, nor limit any other statute or rule of law by reason of which the act of a notary public or commissioner of deeds, or the record thereof, is valid or is deemed valid in any case.

Real Property Law
§290. Definitions; effect of article.
***

3. The term "conveyance" includes every written instrument, by which any estate or interest in real property is created, transferred, mortgaged or assigned, or by which the title to any real property may be affected, including an instrument in execution of power, although the power be one of revocation only, and an instrument postponing or subordinating a mortgage lien; except a will, a lease for a term not exceeding three years, an executory contract for the sale or purchase of lands, and an instrument containing a power to convey real property as the agent or attorney for the owner of such property.

***

§298. Acknowledgments and proofs within the state.

The acknowledgment or proof, within this state, of a conveyance of real property situate in this State may be made:

1. At any place within the state, before

   (a) a justice of the supreme court;

   (b) an official examiner of title;

   (c) an official referee; or

   (d) a notary public.

2. Within the district wherein such officer is authorized to perform official duties, before

   (a) a judge or clerk of any court of record;

   (b) a commissioner of deeds outside of the City of New York, or a commissioner of deeds of the City of New York within the five counties comprising the City of New York;

   (c) the mayor or recorder of a city;

   (d) a surrogate, special surrogate, or special county judge; or

   (e) the county clerk or other recording officer of a county.

3. Before a justice of the peace, town councilman, village police justice or a judge of any court of inferior local jurisdiction, anywhere within the county containing the town, village or city in which he is authorized to perform official duties.

§302. Acknowledgments and proofs by married women.

The acknowledgment or proof of a conveyance of real property, within the state, or of any other written instrument, may be made by a married woman the same as if unmarried.

§303. Requisites of acknowledgments.

An acknowledgment must not be taken by any officer unless he knows or has satisfactory evidence, that the person making it is the person described in and who executed such instrument.

§304. Proof by subscribing witness.

When the execution of a conveyance is proved by a subscribing witness, such witness must state his own place of residence, and if his place of residence is in a city, the street and street number, if any thereof, and that he knew the person described in and who executed the conveyance. The proof must not be taken unless the officer is personally acquainted with such witness, or has satisfactory evidence that he is the same person, who was a subscribing witness to the conveyance.

§306. Certificate of acknowledgment or proof.

A person taking the acknowledgment or proof of a conveyance must endorse thereupon or attach thereto, a certificate, signed by himself, stating all the matters required to be done, known, or proved on the taking of such acknowledgment or proof; together with the name and substance of the testimony of each witness examined before him, and if a subscribing witness, his place of residence.

***

§309-a. Uniform forms of certificates of acknowledgment or proof within this state.

1. The certificate of an acknowledgment, within this State, or a conveyance or other instrument in respect to real property situate in this State, by a person, must conform substantially with the following form, the blanks being properly filled:

State of New York   )
)   ss.:
County of.......   )

On the......day of......in the year......before me, the undersigned, personally appeared ......, personally known to me or proved to me on the basis of satisfactory evidence to be the individual(s) whose name(s) is (are) subscribed to the within instrument and acknowledged to me that he/she/they executed the same in his/her/their capacity (ies), and that by his/her/their signature(s) on the instrument, the individual(s), or the person upon behalf of which the individual(s) acted, executed the instrument. *(Signature and office of individual taking acknowledgment.)*

2. The certificate for a proof of execution by a subscribing witness, within this state, of a conveyance or other instrument made by any person in respect to real property situate in this state, must conform substantially with the following form, the blanks being properly filled:

State of New York   )
)   ss.:
County of.......   )

On the......day of......in the year......before me, the undersigned, personally appeared .... .., the subscribing witness to the foregoing instrument, with whom I am personally acquainted, who, being by me duly sworn, did depose and say that he/she/they reside(s) in......(if the place of residence is in a city, include the street and street number, if any, thereof); that he/she/they know(s)...... to be the individual described in and who executed the foregoing instrument; that said subscribing witness was present and saw said.....execute the same; and that said witness at the same time subscribed his/her/their name(s) as a witness thereto. *(Signature and office of individual taking proof)*.

3. A certificate of an acknowledgment or proof taken under §300 of this article shall include the additional information required by that section.

4. For the purposes of this section, the term "person" means any corporation, joint stock company, estate, general partnership (including any registered limited liability partnership or for-

eign limited liability partnership), limited liability company (including a professional service limited liability company), foreign limited liability company (including a foreign professional service limited liability company), joint venture, limited partnership, natural person, attorney in fact, real estate investment trust, business trust or other trust, custodian, nominee or any other individual or entity in its own or any representative capacity.

§ 309-b. Uniform forms of certificates of acknowledgment or proof without this state.
1. The certificate of an acknowledgment, without this State, of a conveyance or other instrument with respect to real property situate in this State, by a person, may conform substantially with the following form, the blanks being properly filled:

State, District of Columbia,   )
Territory, Possession, or   )   ss.:
Foreign Country.......   )

On the......day of......in the year......before me, the undersigned, personally appeared ......, personally known to me or proved to me on the basis of satisfactory evidence to be the individual(s) whose name(s) is (are) subscribed to the within instrument and acknowledged to me that he/she/they executed the same in his/her/their capacity(ies), and that by his/her/their signature(s) on the instrument, the individual(s), or the person upon behalf of which the individual(s) acted, executed the instrument. *(Signature and office of individual taking acknowledgment.)*

2. The certificate for a proof of execution by a subscribing witness, without this State, of a conveyance or other instrument made by any person in respect to real property situate in this State, may conform substantially with the following form, the blanks being properly filled:

State, District of Columbia,   )
Territory, Possession, or   )   ss.:
Foreign Country.......   )

On the......day of......in the year......before me, the undersigned, personally appeared ......, the subscribing witness to the foregoing instrument, with whom I am personally acquainted, who, being by me duly sworn, did depose and say that he/she resides in......(if the place of residence is in a city, include the street and street number, if any, thereof); that he/she knows......to be the individual described in and who executed the foregoing instrument; that said subscribing witness was present and saw said......execute the same; and that said witness at the same time subscribed his/her name as a witness thereto.
(Signature and office of individual taking proof.)

3. No provision of this section shall be construed to:
(a) modify the choice of laws afforded by §§299-a and 301-a of this article pursuant to which an acknowledgment or proof may be taken;
(b) modify any requirement of §307 of this article;
(c) modify any requirement for a seal imposed by subdivision one of §308 of this article;
(d) modify any requirement concerning a certificate of authentication imposed by §308, 311,312, 314, or 318 of this article; or
(e) modify any requirement imposed by any provision of this article when the certificate of acknowledgment or proof purports to be taken in the manner prescribed by the laws of another state, the District of Columbia, territory, possession, or foreign country.
4. A certificate of an acknowledgment or proof taken under §300 of this article shall include the additional information required by that section.

5. For the purposes of this section, the term "person" means a person as defined in subdivision 4 of §309-a of this article.

6. The inclusion within the body (other than the jurat) of a certificate of acknowledgment or proof made under this section or the city or other political subdivision and the state or country or other place the acknowledgment was taken shall be deemed. A non-substantial variance from the form of a certificate authorized by this section.

§330. Officers guilty of malfeasance liable for damages.

An officer authorized to take the acknowledgment or proof of a conveyance or other instrument, or to certify such proof or acknowledgment, or to record the same, who is guilty of malfeasance or fraudulent practice in the execution of any duty prescribed by law in relation thereto, is liable in damages to the person injured.

§333. When conveyances of real property not to be recorded.

***

2. A recording officer shall not record or accept for record any conveyance of real property, unless said conveyance in its entirety and the certificate of acknowledgment or proof and the authentication thereof, other than proper names therein which may be in another language provided they are written in English letters or characters, shall be in the English language, or unless such conveyance, certificate of acknowledgment or proof, and the authentication thereof be accompanied by and have attached thereto a translation in the English language duly executed and acknowledged by the person or persons making such conveyance and proved and authenticated, if need be, in the manner required of conveyances for recording in this state, or, unless such conveyance, certificate of acknowledgment or proof, and the authentication thereof be accompanied by and have attached thereto a translation in the English language made by a person duly designated for such purpose by the county judge of the county where it is desired to record such conveyance or a justice of the supreme court and be duly signed, acknowledged and certified under oath or upon affirmation by such person before such judge, to be a true and accurate translation and contain a certification of the designation of such person by such judge.

Special Note

By reason of changes in certain provisions of the Real Property Law, any and all limitations on the authority of a notary public to act as such in any part of the State have been removed; a notary public may now, in addition to administering oaths or taking affidavits anywhere in the State, take acknowledgments and proofs of conveyances anywhere in the State. The need for a certificate of authentication of a county clerk as a prerequisite to recording or use in evidence in this State of the instrument acknowledged or proved has been abolished. The certificate of authentication may possibly be required where the instrument is to be recorded or used in evidence outside the jurisdiction of the State.

§335. Banking Law

If the rental fee of any safe deposit box is not paid, or after the termination of the lease for such box, and at least 30 days after giving proper notice to the lessee, the lessor (bank) may, in the presence of a notary public, open the safe deposit box, remove and inventory the contents. The notary public shall then file with the lessor a certificate under seal which states the date of the opening of the safe deposit box, the name of the lessee, and a list of the contents. Within 10 days of the opening of the safe deposit box, a copy of this certificate must be mailed to the lessee at his last known postal address.

Rule 3113. Civil Practice Law and Rules

This rule authorizes a deposition to be taken before a notary public in a civil proceeding.

§11. Domestic Relations Law
A notary public has no authority to solemnize marriages; nor may a notary public take the acknowledgment of parties and witnesses to a written contract of marriage.

§10. Public Officers Law
Official oaths, permits the oath of a public officer to be administered by a notary public.

Restrictions and Violations

Index

Law	Sec	Subject
Judiciary Law	484	None but Attorneys to Practice
Judiciary Law	485	Misdemeanor Violations
Judiciary Law	750	Powers of Courts to Punish
Public Officers Law	15	Notary Must Not Act Before Taking/Filing Oath
Public Officers Law	67	Fees of Public Officers
Public Officers Law	69	Fees Prohibited for Administering Certain Oaths
Executive Law	135a	Removal From Office for Misconduct
Penal Law	70.00	Sentence of Imprisonment for Felony
Penal Law	70.15	Sentences of Imprisonment for Misdemeanors
Penal Law	170.10	Forgery in the Second Degree
Penal Law	175.40	Issuing a False Certificate
Penal Law	195.00	Official Misconduct

Judiciary Law

§484. None but attorneys to practice in the state.
No natural person shall ask or receive, directly or indirectly, compensation for appearing for a person other than himself as attorney in any court or before any magistrate, or for preparing deeds, mortgages, assignments, discharges, leases or any other instruments affecting real estate, wills, codicils, or any other instrument affecting the disposition of property after death, or decedents' estates, or pleadings of any kind in any action brought before any court of record in this state, or make it a business to practice for another as an attorney in any court or before any magistrate unless he has been regularly admitted to practice, as an attorney or counselor, in the courts of record in the state; but nothing in this section shall apply
(1) to officers of societies for the prevention of cruelty, duly appointed, when exercising the special powers conferred upon such corporations under §1403 of the Not-for-Profit Corporation Law; or
(2) to law students who have completed at least 2 semesters of law school or persons who have graduated from a law school, who have taken the examination for admittance to practice law in the courts of record in the state immediately available after graduation from law school, or the examination immediately available after being notified by the board of law examiners that they failed to pass said exam, and who have not been notified by the board of law examiners that they have failed to pass two such examinations, acting under the supervision of a legal aid organization, when such students and persons are acting under a program approved by the appellate division of the supreme court of the department in which the principal office of such organization is

located and specifying the extent to which such students and persons may engage in activities prohibited by this statute; or

(3) to persons who have graduated from a law school approved pursuant to the rules of the court of appeals for the admission of attorneys and counselors-at-law and who have taken the examination for admission to practice as an attorney and counselor-at-law immediately available after graduation from law school or the examination immediately available after being notified by the board of law examiners that they failed to pass said exam, and who have not been notified by the board of law examiners that they have failed to pass two such examinations, when such persons are acting under the supervision of the state or a subdivision thereof or of any officer or agency of the state or a subdivision thereof, pursuant to a program approved by the appellate division of the supreme court of the department within which such activities are taking place and specifying the extent to which they may engage in activities otherwise prohibited by this statute and those powers of the supervising governmental entity or officer in connection with which they may engage in such activities.

§485. Violation of certain preceding sections a misdemeanor.
Any person violating the provisions of §§478, 479, 480, 481, 482, 483 or 484, shall be guilty of a misdemeanor.

§750. Power of courts to punish for criminal contempts.
*** B. *** the supreme court has power under this section to punish for a criminal contempt any person who unlawfully practices or assumes to practice law; and a proceeding under this subdivision may be instituted on the court's own motion or on the motion of any officer charged with the duty of investigating or prosecuting unlawful practice of law, or by any bar association incorporated under the laws of this State.

Illegal practice of law by notary public.
To make it a business to practice as an attorney at law, not being a lawyer, is a crime. "Counsel and advice, the drawing of agreements, the organization of corporations and preparing papers connected therewith, the drafting of legal documents of all kinds, including wills, are activities which have been long classed as law practice." (*People v. Alfani*, 227 NY 334, 339.)

Wills.
The execution of wills under the supervision of a notary public acting in effect as a lawyer, "cannot be too strongly condemned, not only for the reason that it means an invasion of the legal profession, but for the fact that testators thereby run the risk of frustrating their own solemnly declared intentions and rendering worthless maturely considered plans for the disposition of estates whose creation may have been the fruit of lives of industry and self-denial." (*Matter of Flynn*, 142 Misc. 7.)

Public Officers Law
Notary must not act before taking and filing oath of office. The Public Officers Law (§15) provides that a person who executes any of the functions of a public office without having taken and duly filed the required oath of office, as prescribed by law, is guilty of a misdemeanor. A notary public is a public officer.

§67. Fees of public officers.
1. Each public officer upon whom a duty is expressly imposed by law, must execute the same without fee or reward, except where a fee or other compensation therefor is expressly allowed by law.

2. An officer or other person, to whom a fee or other compensation is allowed by law, for any service, shall not charge or receive a greater fee or reward, for that service, than is so allowed.

3. An officer, or other person, shall not demand or receive any fee or compensation, allowed to him by law for any service, unless the service was actually rendered by him; except that an officer may demand in advance his fee, where he is, by law, expressly directed or permitted to require payment thereof, before rendering the service.

4. *** An officer or other person, who violates either of the provisions contained in this section, is liable, in addition to the punishment prescribed by law for the criminal offense, to an action in behalf of the person aggrieved, in which the plaintiff is entitled to treble damages.

A notary public subjects himself to criminal prosecution, civil suit and possible removal by asking or receiving more than the statutory allowance, for administering the ordinary oath in connect with an affidavit. (Op. Atty. Gen. (1917) 12 St. Dept. Rep. 507.)

§69. Fee for administering certain official oaths prohibited.

An officer is not entitled to a fee, for administering the oath of office to a member of the legislature, to any military officer, to an inspector of election, clerk of the poll, or to any other public officer or public employee.

Executive Law

Misconduct by a notary and removal from office.

A notary public who, in the performance of the duties of such office shall practice any fraud or deceit, is guilty of a misdemeanor (Executive Law, §135-a), and may be removed from office. The notary may be removed from office if the notary made a misstatement of a material fact in his application for appointment; for preparing and taking an oath of an affiant to a statement that the notary knew to be false or fraudulent.

Penal Law

§70.00 Sentence of imprisonment for felony.
***

2. Maximum term of sentence. The maximum term of an indeterminate sentence shall be at least three years and the term shall be fixed as follows:
***

(d) For a class D felony, the term shall be fixed by the court, and shall not exceed 7 years; and
(e) For a class E felony, the term shall be fixed by the court, and shall not exceed 4 years.
***

§70.15 Sentences of imprisonment for misdemeanors and violation.

1. Class A misdemeanor. A sentence of imprisonment for a class A misdemeanor shall be a definite sentence. When such a sentence is imposed the term shall be fixed by the court, and shall not exceed one year; ***

§170.10 Forgery in the second degree.

A person is guilty of forgery in the second degree when, with intent to defraud, deceive or injure another, he falsely makes, completes or alters a written instrument which is or purports to be, or which is calculated to become or to represent if completed:

1. A deed, will, codicil, contract, assignment, commercial instrument, or other instrument which does or may evidence, create, transfer, terminate or otherwise affect a legal right, interest, obligation or status; or

2. A public record, or an instrument filed or required or authorized by law to be filed in or with a public office or public servant; or

3. A written instrument officially issued or created by a public office, public servant or governmental instrumentality.

***

Forgery in the second degree is a class D felony.

§175.40 Issuing a false certificate.

A person is guilty of issuing a false certificate when, being a public servant authorized by law to make or issue official certificates or other official written instruments, and with intent to defraud, deceive or injure another person, he issues such an instrument, or makes the same with intent that it be issued, knowing that it contains a false statement or false information.

Issuing a false certificate is a class E felony.

§195.00 Official misconduct.

A public servant is guilty of official misconduct when, with intent to obtain a benefit or to injure or deprive another person of a benefit:

1. He commits an act relating to his office but constituting an unauthorized exercise of his official functions, knowing that such act is unauthorized; or
2. He knowingly refrains from performing a duty which is imposed upon him by law or is clearly inherent in the nature of his office.

Official misconduct is a class A misdemeanor.

Notary must officiate on request.

The Penal Law (§195.00) provides that an officer before whom an oath or affidavit may be taken is bound to administer the same when requested, and a refusal to do so is a misdemeanor. (People v. Brooks, 1 Den. 457.)

Perjury.

One is guilty of perjury if he has stated or given testimony on a material matter, under oath or by affirmation, as to the truth thereof, when he knew the statement or testimony to be false and willfully made.

Definitions and General Terms

Acknowledgment

A formal declaration before a duly authorized officer by a person who has executed an instrument that such execution is his act and deed. Technically, an "acknowledgment" is the declaration of a person described in and who has executed a written instrument, that he executed the same. As commonly used, the term means the certificate of an officer, duly empowered to take an acknowledgment or proof of the conveyance of real property, that **on a specified date "before me came...................., to me known to be the individual described in and who executed the foregoing instrument and acknowledged that he executed the same."** The purposes of the law respecting acknowledgments are not only to promote the security of land titles and to prevent frauds in conveyancing, but to furnish proof of the due execution of conveyances (*Armstrong v. Combs*, 15 App. Div. 246) so as to permit the document to be given in evidence, without further proof of its execution, and make it a recordable instrument.

The Real Property Law prescribes:

"**§303. Requisites of acknowledgments.** An acknowledgment must not be taken by any officer unless he knows or has satisfactory evidence, that the person making it is the person described in and who executed such instrument."

The thing to be known is the identity of the person making the acknowledgment with the person described in the instrument and the person who executed the same. This knowledge must be possessed by the notary (*Gross v. Rowley*, 147 App. Div. 529), and a notary must not take an acknowledgment unless the notary knows or has proof that the person making it is the person described in and who executed the instrument (*People v. Kempner*, 49 App. Div. 121). It is not essential that the person who executed the instrument sign his name in the presence of the notary.

Taking acknowledgments over the telephone is illegal and a notary public is guilty of a misdemeanor in so acting. **In the certificate of acknowledgment a notary public declares: "On this.......day of.............20......., before me came...............to me known," etc.** Unless the person purporting to have made the acknowledgment actually and personally appeared before the notary on the day specified, the notary's certificate that he so came is palpably false and fraudulent. (*Matter of Brooklyn Bar Assoc.*, 225 App. Div. 680.)

Interest as a disqualification.
A notary public should not take an acknowledgment to a legal instrument to which the notary is a party in interest. (*Armstrong v. Combs*, 15 App. Div. 246.)

Fraudulent certificates of acknowledgment.
A notary public who knowingly makes a false certificate that a deed or other written instrument was acknowledged by a party thereto is guilty of forgery in the second degree, which is punishable by imprisonment for a term of not exceeding 7 years (Penal Law, §§170.10 and 70.00[2(d)]. The essence of the crime is false certification, intention to defraud. (*People v. Abeel*, 182 NY 415.) While the absence of guilty knowledge or criminal intent would absolve the notary from criminal liability, the conveyance, of which the false certification is an essential part, is a forgery and, therefore, invalid. (*Caccioppoli v. Lemmo*, 152 App. Div. 650.)

Damages recoverable from notary for false certificate.
Action for damages sustained where notary certified that mortgagor had appeared and acknowledged a mortgage. (*Kainz v. Goldsmith*, 231 App. Div. 171.)

Administrator
A person appointed by the court to manage the estate of a deceased person who left no will.

Affiant
The person who makes and subscribes his signature to an affidavit.

Affidavit
An affidavit is a signed statement, duly sworn to, by the maker thereof, before a notary public or other officer authorized to administer oaths. The venue, or county wherein the affidavit was sworn to should be accurately stated. But it is of far more importance that the affiant, the person making the affidavit, should have personally appeared before the notary and have made oath to the statements contained in the affidavit as required by law. Under the Penal Law (§210.00) the wilful making of a false affidavit is perjury, but to sustain an indictment therefor, there must have been, in some form, in the presence of an officer authorized to administer an oath, an unequivocal and present act by which the affiant consciously took upon himself the obligation of an oath; his silent delivery of a signed affidavit to the notary for his certificate, is not enough. (*People v. O'Reilly*, 86 NY 154; People ex rel. *Greene v. Swasey*, 122 Misc. 388; *People v. Levitas* (1963) 40 Misc. 2d 331.) A notary public will be removed from office for preparing and taking the oath of an affiant to a statement that the notary knew to be false. (*Matter of Senft*, August 8, 1929; *Matter of Trotta*, February 20, 1930; *Matter of Kibbe*, December 24, 1931.)

The distinction between the taking of an acknowledgment and an affidavit must be clearly undestood. In the case of an acknowledgment, the notary public certifies as to the identity

and execution of a document; the affidavit involves the administration of an oath to the affiant. **There are certain acknowledgment forms which are a combination of an acknowledgment and affidavit.** It is incumbent on the notary public to scrutinize each document presented to him and to ascertain the exact nature of the notary's duty with relation thereto. An affidavit differs from a deposition in that an affidavit is an ex parte statement. (See definition of Deposition.)

Affirmation
A solemn declaration made by persons who conscientiously decline taking an oath; it is equivalent to an oath and is just as binding; if a person has religious or conscientious scruples against taking an oath, the notary public should have the person affirm. **The following is a form of affirmation: "Do you solemnly, sincerely, and truly, declare and affirm that the statements made by you are true and correct."**

Apostile
Department of State authentication attached to a notarized and county-certified document for possible international use.

Attest
To witness the execution of a written instrument, at the request of the person who makes it, and subscribe the same as a witness.

Attestation Clause
That clause (e.g., at the end of a will) wherein the witnesses certify that the instrument has been executed before them, and the manner of the execution of the same.

Authentication (Notarial)
A certificate subjoined by a county clerk to any certificate of proof or acknowledgment or oath signed by a notary; this county clerk's certificate authenticates or verifies the authority of the notary public to act as such. (See §133, Executive Law.)

Bill of Sale
A written instrument given to pass title of personal property from vendor to vendee.

Certified Copy
A copy of a public record signed and certified as a true copy by the public official having custody of the original. A notary public has no authority to issue certified copies. Notaries must not certify to the authenticity of legal documents and other papers required to be filed with foreign consular officers. Within this prohibition are certificates of the following type:

United States of America)
State of New York) ss.:
County of New York)

"I..............., a notary public of the State of New York, in and for the county of.........., duly commissioned, qualified and sworn according to the laws of the State of New York, do hereby certify and declare that I verily believe the annexed instrument executed by.......and sworn to before.........., a notary public of the State of.........., to be genuine in every respect, and that full faith and credit are and ought to be given thereto.

"In testimony whereof I have hereunto set my hand and seal at the City of ...., this .... day of ...., 20........
(Seal) (Notarial Signature.)"

Chattel
Personal property, such as household goods or fixtures.

Chattel Paper
A writing or writings which evidence both an obligation to pay money and a security interest in a lease or specific goods. The agreement which creates or provides for the security interest is known as a security agreement.

Codicil
An instrument made subsequent to a will and modifying it in some respects.

Consideration
Anything of value given to induce entering into a contract; it may be money, personal services, or even love and affection.

Contempt of Court
Behavior disrespectful of the authority of a court which disrupts the execution of court orders.

Contract
An agreement between competent parties to do or not to do certain things for a legal consideration, whereby each party acquires a right to what the other possesses.

Conveyance (Deed)
Every instrument, in writing, except a will, by which any estate or interest in real property is created, transferred, assigned or surrendered.

County Clerk's Certificate
See "Authentication (Notarial)."

Deponent
One who makes oath to a written statement. Technically, a person subscribing a deposition but used interchangeably with "Affiant."

Deposition
The testimony of a witness taken out of court or other hearing proceeding, under oath or by affirmation, before a notary public or other person, officer or commissioner before whom such testimony is authorized by law to be taken, which is intended to be used at the trial or hearing.

Duress
Unlawful constraint exercised upon a person whereby he is forced to do some act against his will.

Escrow
The placing of an instrument in the hands of a person as a depository who on the happening of a designated event, is to deliver the instrument to a third person. This agreement, once established, should be unalterable.

Executor
One named in a will to carry out the provisions of the will.

Ex Parte (From One Side Only)
A hearing or examination in the presence of, or on papers filed by, one party and in the absence of the other.

Felony
A crime punishable by death or imprisonment in a state prison.

Guardian
A person in charge of a minor's person or property.

Judgment
Decree of a court declaring that one individual is indebted to another and fixing the amount of such indebtedness.

Jurat
A jurat is that part of an affidavit where the officer (notary public) certifies that it was sworn to before him. It is not the affidavit.
The following is the form of jurat generally employed:
"Sworn to before me this........day of........, 20......"
Those words placed directly after the signature in the affidavit stating that the facts therein contained were sworn to or affirmed before the *officer* (notary public) together with his official signature and such other data as required by § 137 of the Executive Law.

Laches
The delay or negligence in asserting one's legal rights.

Lease
A contract whereby, for a consideration, usually termed rent, one who is entitled to the possession of real property transfers such right to another for life, for a term of years or at will.

Lien
A legal right or claim upon a specific property which attaches to the property until a debt is satisfied.

Litigation
The act of carrying on a lawsuit.

Misdemeanor
Any crime other than a felony.

Mortgage On Real Property
An instrument in writing, duly executed and delivered that creates a lien upon real estate as security for the payment of a specified debt, which is usually in the form of a bond.

Notary Public
A public officer who executes acknowledgments of deeds or writings in order to render them available as evidence of the facts therein contained; administers oaths and affirmation as to the truth of statements contained in papers or documents requiring the administration of an oath. The notary's general authority is defined in § 135 of the Executive Law; the notary has certain other powers which can be found in the various provisions of law set forth earlier in this publication.

Oath
A verbal pledge given by the person taking it that his statements are made under an immediate sense of this responsibility to God, who will punish the affiant if the statements are false.
Notaries public must administer oaths and affirmations in manner and form as prescribed by the Civil Practice Law and Rules, namely:
§2309(b) Form. An oath or affirmation shall be administered in a form calculated to awaken the conscience and impress the mind of the person taking it in accordance with his religious or ethical beliefs.
An oath must be administered as required by law. The person taking the oath must personally appear before the notary; an oath cannot be administered over the telephone (Matter of Napolis, 169 App. Div. 469), and the oath must be administered in the form required by the statute (Bookman v. City of New York, 200 NY 53, 56).

When an oath is administered the person taking the oath must express assent to the oath repeated by thenotary by the words "I do" or some other words of like meaning.

For an oath or affirmation to be valid, whatever form is adopted, it is necessary that: first, the person swearing or affirming must personally be in the presence of the notary public; secondly, that the person unequivocally swears or affirms that what he states is true; thirdly, that he swears or affirms as of that time; and, lastly, that the person conscientiously takes upon himself the obligation of an oath.

A notary public does not fulfill his duty by merely asking a person whether the signature on a purported affidavit is his. An oath must be administered.

A corporation or a partnership cannot take an oath; an oath must be taken by an individual.

A notary public cannot administer an oath to himself.

The privileges and rights of a notary public are personal and cannot be delegated to anyone.

Plaintiff
A person who starts a suit or brings an action against another.

Power of Attorney
A written statement by an individual giving another person the power to act for him.

Proof
The formal declaration made by a subscribing witness to the execution of an instrument setting forth his place of residence, that he knew the person described in and who executed the instrument and that he saw such person execute such instrument.

Protest
A formal statement in writing by a notary public, under seal, that a certain bill of exchange or promissory note was on a certain day presented for payment, or acceptance, and that such payment or acceptance was refused.

Seal
The laws of the State of New York do not require the use of seals by notaries public. If a seal is used, it should sufficiently identify the notary public, his authority and jurisdiction. It is the opinion of the Department of State that the only inscription required is the name of the notary and the words "Notary Public for the State of New York."

Signature of Notary Public
A notary public must sign the name under which he was appointed and no other. In addition to his signature and venue, the notary public shall print, typewrite or stamp beneath his signature in black ink, his name, the words "Notary Public State of New York," the name of the county in which he is qualified, and the date upon which his commission expires (§137, Executive Law).

When a woman notary marries during the term of office for which she was appointed, she may continue to use her maiden name as notary public. However, if she elects to use her marriage name, then for the balance of her term as a notary public she must continue to use her maiden name in her signature and seal when acting in her notarial capacity, adding after her signature her married name, in parentheses. When renewing her commission as a notary public, she may apply under her married name or her maiden name. She must then perform all her notarial functions under the name selected. A member of a religious order, known therein by a name other than his secular cognomen, may be appointed and may officiate as a notary public under the name by which he is known in religious circles. (Op. Atty. Gen., Mar. 20, 1930.)

Statute
A law established by an act of the Legislature.

Statute of Frauds
State law which provides that certain contracts must be in writing or partially complied with, in order to be enforceable at law.

Statute of Limitations
A law that limits the time within which a criminal prosecution or a civil action must be started.

Subordination Clause
A clause which permits the placing of a mortgage at a later date which takes priority over an existing mortgage.

Sunday
A notary public may administer an oath or take an affidavit or acknowledgment on Sunday. However, a deposition cannot be taken on Sunday in a civil proceeding.

Swear
This term includes every mode authorized by law for administering an oath.

Taking an Acknowledgment
The act of the person named in an instrument telling the notary public that he is the person named in the instrument and acknowledging that he executed such instrument; also includes the act of the notary public in obtaining satisfactory evidence of the identity of the person whose acknowledgment is taken. The notary public "certifies to the taking of the acknowledgment" when the notary signs his official signature to the form setting forth the fact of the taking of the acknowledgment.

Venue
The geographical place where a notary public takes an affidavit or acknowledgment. Every affidavit or certificate of acknowledgment should show on its face the venue of the notarial act. The venue is usually set forth at the beginning of the instrument or at the top of the notary's jurat, or official certification, as follows: "State of New York, County of (New York) ss.:". Section 137 of the Executive Law imposes the duty on the notary public to include the venue of his act in all certificates of acknowledgments or jurats to affidavits.

Will
The disposition of one's property to take effect after death.

Schedule of Fees

Appointment as Notary Public-	
Total Commission Fee	$60.00
($40 appointment and $20 filing of Oath of Office)	
Change of Name/Address	10.00
Duplicate Identification Card	10.00
Issuance of Certificate of Official Character	5.00
Filing Certificate of Official Character	10.00
Authentication Certificate	3.00
Protest of Note, Commercial Paper, etc.	.75
Each additional Notice of Protest (limit 5) each	.10

Oath or Affirmation	2.00
Acknowledgment (each person)	2.00
Proof of Execution (each person)	2.00
Swearing Witness	2.00

Note
Where gender pronouns appear in this booklet, they are meant to refer to both male and female persons.

HOW TO TAKE A TEST

I. YOU MUST PASS AN EXAMINATION

A. *WHAT EVERY CANDIDATE SHOULD KNOW*

Examination applicants often ask us for help in preparing for the written test. What can I study in advance? What kinds of questions will be asked? How will the test be given? How will the papers be graded?

As an applicant for a civil service examination, you may be wondering about some of these things. Our purpose here is to suggest effective methods of advance study and to describe civil service examinations.

Your chances for success on this examination can be increased if you know how to prepare. Those "pre-examination jitters" can be reduced if you know what to expect. You can even experience an adventure in good citizenship if you know why civil service exams are given.

B. *WHY ARE CIVIL SERVICE EXAMINATIONS GIVEN?*

Civil service examinations are important to you in two ways. As a citizen, you want public jobs filled by employees who know how to do their work. As a job seeker, you want a fair chance to compete for that job on an equal footing with other candidates. The best-known means of accomplishing this two-fold goal is the competitive examination.

Exams are widely publicized throughout the nation. They may be administered for jobs in federal, state, city, municipal, town or village governments or agencies.

Any citizen may apply, with some limitations, such as the age or residence of applicants. Your experience and education may be reviewed to see whether you meet the requirements for the particular examination. When these requirements exist, they are reasonable and applied consistently to all applicants. Thus, a competitive examination may cause you some uneasiness now, but it is your privilege and safeguard.

C. *HOW ARE CIVIL SERVICE EXAMS DEVELOPED?*

Examinations are carefully written by trained technicians who are specialists in the field known as "psychological measurement," in consultation with recognized authorities in the field of work that the test will cover. These experts recommend the subject matter areas or skills to be tested; only those knowledges or skills important to your success on the job are included. The most reliable books and source materials available are used as references. Together, the experts and technicians judge the difficulty level of the questions.

Test technicians know how to phrase questions so that the problem is clearly stated. Their ethics do not permit "trick" or "catch" questions. Questions may have been tried out on sample groups, or subjected to statistical analysis, to determine their usefulness.

Written tests are often used in combination with performance tests, ratings of training and experience, and oral interviews. All of these measures combine to form the best-known means of finding the right person for the right job.

II. HOW TO PASS THE WRITTEN TEST

A. NATURE OF THE EXAMINATION

To prepare intelligently for civil service examinations, you should know how they differ from school examinations you have taken. In school you were assigned certain definite pages to read or subjects to cover. The examination questions were quite detailed and usually emphasized memory. Civil service exams, on the other hand, try to discover your present ability to perform the duties of a position, plus your potentiality to learn these duties. In other words, a civil service exam attempts to predict how successful you will be. Questions cover such a broad area that they cannot be as minute and detailed as school exam questions.

In the public service similar kinds of work, or positions, are grouped together in one "class." This process is known as *position-classification*. All the positions in a class are paid according to the salary range for that class. One class title covers all of these positions, and they are all tested by the same examination.

B. FOUR BASIC STEPS

1) Study the announcement

How, then, can you know what subjects to study? Our best answer is: "Learn as much as possible about the class of positions for which you've applied." The exam will test the knowledge, skills and abilities needed to do the work.

Your most valuable source of information about the position you want is the official exam announcement. This announcement lists the training and experience qualifications. Check these standards and apply only if you come reasonably close to meeting them.

The brief description of the position in the examination announcement offers some clues to the subjects which will be tested. Think about the job itself. Review the duties in your mind. Can you perform them, or are there some in which you are rusty? Fill in the blank spots in your preparation.

Many jurisdictions preview the written test in the exam announcement by including a section called "Knowledge and Abilities Required," "Scope of the Examination," or some similar heading. Here you will find out specifically what fields will be tested.

2) Review your own background

Once you learn in general what the position is all about, and what you need to know to do the work, ask yourself which subjects you already know fairly well and which need improvement. You may wonder whether to concentrate on improving your strong areas or on building some background in your fields of weakness. When the announcement has specified "some knowledge" or "considerable knowledge," or has used adjectives like "beginning principles of..." or "advanced ... methods," you can get a clue as to the number and difficulty of questions to be asked in any given field. More questions, and hence broader coverage, would be included for those subjects which are more important in the work. Now weigh your strengths and weaknesses against the job requirements and prepare accordingly.

3) Determine the level of the position

Another way to tell how intensively you should prepare is to understand the level of the job for which you are applying. Is it the entering level? In other words, is this the position in which beginners in a field of work are hired? Or is it an intermediate or advanced level? Sometimes this is indicated by such words as "Junior" or "Senior" in the class title. Other jurisdictions use Roman numerals to designate the level – Clerk I, Clerk II, for example. The word "Supervisor" sometimes appears in the title. If the level is not indicated by the title, check the description of duties. Will you be working under very close supervision, or will you have responsibility for independent decisions in this work?

4) Choose appropriate study materials

Now that you know the subjects to be examined and the relative amount of each subject to be covered, you can choose suitable study materials. For beginning level jobs, or even advanced ones, if you have a pronounced weakness in some aspect of your training, read a modern, standard textbook in that field. Be sure it is up to date and has general coverage. Such books are normally available at your library, and the librarian will be glad to help you locate one. For entry-level positions, questions of appropriate difficulty are chosen – neither highly advanced questions, nor those too simple. Such questions require careful thought but not advanced training.

If the position for which you are applying is technical or advanced, you will read more advanced, specialized material. If you are already familiar with the basic principles of your field, elementary textbooks would waste your time. Concentrate on advanced textbooks and technical periodicals. Think through the concepts and review difficult problems in your field.

These are all general sources. You can get more ideas on your own initiative, following these leads. For example, training manuals and publications of the government agency which employs workers in your field can be useful, particularly for technical and professional positions. A letter or visit to the government department involved may result in more specific study suggestions, and certainly will provide you with a more definite idea of the exact nature of the position you are seeking.

III. KINDS OF TESTS

Tests are used for purposes other than measuring knowledge and ability to perform specified duties. For some positions, it is equally important to test ability to make adjustments to new situations or to profit from training. In others, basic mental abilities not dependent on information are essential. Questions which test these things may not appear as pertinent to the duties of the position as those which test for knowledge and information. Yet they are often highly important parts of a fair examination. For very general questions, it is almost impossible to help you direct your study efforts. What we can do is to point out some of the more common of these general abilities needed in public service positions and describe some typical questions.

1) General information

Broad, general information has been found useful for predicting job success in some kinds of work. This is tested in a variety of ways, from vocabulary lists to questions about current events. Basic background in some field of work, such as sociology or economics, may be sampled in a group of questions. Often these are principles which have become familiar to most persons through exposure rather than through formal training. It is difficult to advise you how to study for these questions; being alert to the world around you is our best suggestion.

2) Verbal ability

An example of an ability needed in many positions is verbal or language ability. Verbal ability is, in brief, the ability to use and understand words. Vocabulary and grammar tests are typical measures of this ability. Reading comprehension or paragraph interpretation questions are common in many kinds of civil service tests. You are given a paragraph of written material and asked to find its central meaning.

3) Numerical ability
Number skills can be tested by the familiar arithmetic problem, by checking paired lists of numbers to see which are alike and which are different, or by interpreting charts and graphs. In the latter test, a graph may be printed in the test booklet which you are asked to use as the basis for answering questions.

4) Observation
A popular test for law-enforcement positions is the observation test. A picture is shown to you for several minutes, then taken away. Questions about the picture test your ability to observe both details and larger elements.

5) Following directions
In many positions in the public service, the employee must be able to carry out written instructions dependably and accurately. You may be given a chart with several columns, each column listing a variety of information. The questions require you to carry out directions involving the information given in the chart.

6) Skills and aptitudes
Performance tests effectively measure some manual skills and aptitudes. When the skill is one in which you are trained, such as typing or shorthand, you can practice. These tests are often very much like those given in business school or high school courses. For many of the other skills and aptitudes, however, no short-time preparation can be made. Skills and abilities natural to you or that you have developed throughout your lifetime are being tested.

Many of the general questions just described provide all the data needed to answer the questions and ask you to use your reasoning ability to find the answers. Your best preparation for these tests, as well as for tests of facts and ideas, is to be at your physical and mental best. You, no doubt, have your own methods of getting into an exam-taking mood and keeping "in shape." The next section lists some ideas on this subject.

IV. KINDS OF QUESTIONS

Only rarely is the "essay" question, which you answer in narrative form, used in civil service tests. Civil service tests are usually of the short-answer type. Full instructions for answering these questions will be given to you at the examination. But in case this is your first experience with short-answer questions and separate answer sheets, here is what you need to know:

1) Multiple-choice Questions
Most popular of the short-answer questions is the "multiple choice" or "best answer" question. It can be used, for example, to test for factual knowledge, ability to solve problems or judgment in meeting situations found at work.
A multiple-choice question is normally one of three types—
- It can begin with an incomplete statement followed by several possible endings. You are to find the one ending which *best* completes the statement, although some of the others may not be entirely wrong.
- It can also be a complete statement in the form of a question which is answered by choosing one of the statements listed.

- It can be in the form of a problem – again you select the best answer.

Here is an example of a multiple-choice question with a discussion which should give you some clues as to the method for choosing the right answer:

When an employee has a complaint about his assignment, the action which will *best* help him overcome his difficulty is to
  A. discuss his difficulty with his coworkers
  B. take the problem to the head of the organization
  C. take the problem to the person who gave him the assignment
  D. say nothing to anyone about his complaint

In answering this question, you should study each of the choices to find which is best. Consider choice "A" – Certainly an employee may discuss his complaint with fellow employees, but no change or improvement can result, and the complaint remains unresolved. Choice "B" is a poor choice since the head of the organization probably does not know what assignment you have been given, and taking your problem to him is known as "going over the head" of the supervisor. The supervisor, or person who made the assignment, is the person who can clarify it or correct any injustice. Choice "C" is, therefore, correct. To say nothing, as in choice "D," is unwise. Supervisors have and interest in knowing the problems employees are facing, and the employee is seeking a solution to his problem.

2) True/False Questions

The "true/false" or "right/wrong" form of question is sometimes used. Here a complete statement is given. Your job is to decide whether the statement is right or wrong.

SAMPLE: A roaming cell-phone call to a nearby city costs less than a non-roaming call to a distant city.

This statement is wrong, or false, since roaming calls are more expensive.

This is not a complete list of all possible question forms, although most of the others are variations of these common types. You will always get complete directions for answering questions. Be sure you understand *how* to mark your answers – ask questions until you do.

V. RECORDING YOUR ANSWERS

Computer terminals are used more and more today for many different kinds of exams.
For an examination with very few applicants, you may be told to record your answers in the test booklet itself. Separate answer sheets are much more common. If this separate answer sheet is to be scored by machine – and this is often the case – it is highly important that you mark your answers correctly in order to get credit.
An electronic scoring machine is often used in civil service offices because of the speed with which papers can be scored. Machine-scored answer sheets must be marked with a pencil, which will be given to you. This pencil has a high graphite content which responds to the electronic scoring machine. As a matter of fact, stray dots may register as answers, so do not let your pencil rest on the answer sheet while you are pondering the correct answer. Also, if your pencil lead breaks or is otherwise defective, ask for another.

Since the answer sheet will be dropped in a slot in the scoring machine, be careful not to bend the corners or get the paper crumpled.

The answer sheet normally has five vertical columns of numbers, with 30 numbers to a column. These numbers correspond to the question numbers in your test booklet. After each number, going across the page are four or five pairs of dotted lines. These short dotted lines have small letters or numbers above them. The first two pairs may also have a "T" or "F" above the letters. This indicates that the first two pairs only are to be used if the questions are of the true-false type. If the questions are multiple choice, disregard the "T" and "F" and pay attention only to the small letters or numbers.

Answer your questions in the manner of the sample that follows:

32. The largest city in the United States is
    A. Washington, D.C.
    B. New York City
    C. Chicago
    D. Detroit
    E. San Francisco

1) Choose the answer you think is best. (New York City is the largest, so "B" is correct.)
2) Find the row of dotted lines numbered the same as the question you are answering. (Find row number 32)
3) Find the pair of dotted lines corresponding to the answer. (Find the pair of lines under the mark "B.")
4) Make a solid black mark between the dotted lines.

VI. BEFORE THE TEST

Common sense will help you find procedures to follow to get ready for an examination. Too many of us, however, overlook these sensible measures. Indeed, nervousness and fatigue have been found to be the most serious reasons why applicants fail to do their best on civil service tests. Here is a list of reminders:

- Begin your preparation early – Don't wait until the last minute to go scurrying around for books and materials or to find out what the position is all about.
- Prepare continuously – An hour a night for a week is better than an all-night cram session. This has been definitely established. What is more, a night a week for a month will return better dividends than crowding your study into a shorter period of time.
- Locate the place of the exam – You have been sent a notice telling you when and where to report for the examination. If the location is in a different town or otherwise unfamiliar to you, it would be well to inquire the best route and learn something about the building.
- Relax the night before the test – Allow your mind to rest. Do not study at all that night. Plan some mild recreation or diversion; then go to bed early and get a good night's sleep.
- Get up early enough to make a leisurely trip to the place for the test – This way unforeseen events, traffic snarls, unfamiliar buildings, etc. will not upset you.
- Dress comfortably – A written test is not a fashion show. You will be known by number and not by name, so wear something comfortable.

- Leave excess paraphernalia at home – Shopping bags and odd bundles will get in your way. You need bring only the items mentioned in the official notice you received; usually everything you need is provided. Do not bring reference books to the exam. They will only confuse those last minutes and be taken away from you when in the test room.
- Arrive somewhat ahead of time – If because of transportation schedules you must get there very early, bring a newspaper or magazine to take your mind off yourself while waiting.
- Locate the examination room – When you have found the proper room, you will be directed to the seat or part of the room where you will sit. Sometimes you are given a sheet of instructions to read while you are waiting. Do not fill out any forms until you are told to do so; just read them and be prepared.
- Relax and prepare to listen to the instructions
- If you have any physical problem that may keep you from doing your best, be sure to tell the test administrator. If you are sick or in poor health, you really cannot do your best on the exam. You can come back and take the test some other time.

VII. AT THE TEST

The day of the test is here and you have the test booklet in your hand. The temptation to get going is very strong. Caution! There is more to success than knowing the right answers. You must know how to identify your papers and understand variations in the type of short-answer question used in this particular examination. Follow these suggestions for maximum results from your efforts:

1) Cooperate with the monitor

The test administrator has a duty to create a situation in which you can be as much at ease as possible. He will give instructions, tell you when to begin, check to see that you are marking your answer sheet correctly, and so on. He is not there to guard you, although he will see that your competitors do not take unfair advantage. He wants to help you do your best.

2) Listen to all instructions

Don't jump the gun! Wait until you understand all directions. In most civil service tests you get more time than you need to answer the questions. So don't be in a hurry. Read each word of instructions until you clearly understand the meaning. Study the examples, listen to all announcements and follow directions. Ask questions if you do not understand what to do.

3) Identify your papers

Civil service exams are usually identified by number only. You will be assigned a number; you must not put your name on your test papers. Be sure to copy your number correctly. Since more than one exam may be given, copy your exact examination title.

4) Plan your time

Unless you are told that a test is a "speed" or "rate of work" test, speed itself is usually not important. Time enough to answer all the questions will be provided, but this does not mean that you have all day. An overall time limit has been set. Divide the total time (in minutes) by the number of questions to determine the approximate time you have for each question.

5) Do not linger over difficult questions

If you come across a difficult question, mark it with a paper clip (useful to have along) and come back to it when you have been through the booklet. One caution if you do this – be sure to skip a number on your answer sheet as well. Check often to be sure that you have not lost your place and that you are marking in the row numbered the same as the question you are answering.

6) Read the questions

Be sure you know what the question asks! Many capable people are unsuccessful because they failed to *read* the questions correctly.

7) Answer all questions

Unless you have been instructed that a penalty will be deducted for incorrect answers, it is better to guess than to omit a question.

8) Speed tests

It is often better NOT to guess on speed tests. It has been found that on timed tests people are tempted to spend the last few seconds before time is called in marking answers at random – without even reading them – in the hope of picking up a few extra points. To discourage this practice, the instructions may warn you that your score will be "corrected" for guessing. That is, a penalty will be applied. The incorrect answers will be deducted from the correct ones, or some other penalty formula will be used.

9) Review your answers

If you finish before time is called, go back to the questions you guessed or omitted to give them further thought. Review other answers if you have time.

10) Return your test materials

If you are ready to leave before others have finished or time is called, take ALL your materials to the monitor and leave quietly. Never take any test material with you. The monitor can discover whose papers are not complete, and taking a test booklet may be grounds for disqualification.

VIII. EXAMINATION TECHNIQUES

1) Read the general instructions carefully. These are usually printed on the first page of the exam booklet. As a rule, these instructions refer to the timing of the examination; the fact that you should not start work until the signal and must stop work at a signal, etc. If there are any *special* instructions, such as a choice of questions to be answered, make sure that you note this instruction carefully.

2) When you are ready to start work on the examination, that is as soon as the signal has been given, read the instructions to each question booklet, underline any key words or phrases, such as *least, best, outline, describe* and the like. In this way you will tend to answer as requested rather than discover on reviewing your paper that you *listed without describing*, that you selected the *worst* choice rather than the *best* choice, etc.

3) If the examination is of the objective or multiple-choice type – that is, each question will also give a series of possible answers: A, B, C or D, and you are called upon to select the best answer and write the letter next to that answer on your answer paper – it is advisable to start answering each question in turn. There may be anywhere from 50 to 100 such questions in the three or four hours allotted and you can see how much time would be taken if you read through all the questions before beginning to answer any. Furthermore, if you come across a question or group of questions which you know would be difficult to answer, it would undoubtedly affect your handling of all the other questions.

4) If the examination is of the essay type and contains but a few questions, it is a moot point as to whether you should read all the questions before starting to answer any one. Of course, if you are given a choice – say five out of seven and the like – then it is essential to read all the questions so you can eliminate the two that are most difficult. If, however, you are asked to answer all the questions, there may be danger in trying to answer the easiest one first because you may find that you will spend too much time on it. The best technique is to answer the first question, then proceed to the second, etc.

5) Time your answers. Before the exam begins, write down the time it started, then add the time allowed for the examination and write down the time it must be completed, then divide the time available somewhat as follows:
   - If 3-1/2 hours are allowed, that would be 210 minutes. If you have 80 objective-type questions, that would be an average of 2-1/2 minutes per question. Allow yourself no more than 2 minutes per question, or a total of 160 minutes, which will permit about 50 minutes to review.
   - If for the time allotment of 210 minutes there are 7 essay questions to answer, that would average about 30 minutes a question. Give yourself only 25 minutes per question so that you have about 35 minutes to review.

6) The most important instruction is to *read each question* and make sure you know what is wanted. The second most important instruction is to *time yourself properly* so that you answer every question. The third most important instruction is to *answer every question*. Guess if you have to but include something for each question. Remember that you will receive no credit for a blank and will probably receive some credit if you write something in answer to an essay question. If you guess a letter – say "B" for a multiple-choice question – you may have guessed right. If you leave a blank as an answer to a multiple-choice question, the examiners may respect your feelings but it will not add a point to your score. Some exams may penalize you for wrong answers, so in such cases *only*, you may not want to guess unless you have some basis for your answer.

7) Suggestions
   a. Objective-type questions
      1. Examine the question booklet for proper sequence of pages and questions
      2. Read all instructions carefully
      3. Skip any question which seems too difficult; return to it after all other questions have been answered
      4. Apportion your time properly; do not spend too much time on any single question or group of questions

5. Note and underline key words – *all, most, fewest, least, best, worst, same, opposite*, etc.
6. Pay particular attention to negatives
7. Note unusual option, e.g., unduly long, short, complex, different or similar in content to the body of the question
8. Observe the use of "hedging" words – *probably, may, most likely*, etc.
9. Make sure that your answer is put next to the same number as the question
10. Do not second-guess unless you have good reason to believe the second answer is definitely more correct
11. Cross out original answer if you decide another answer is more accurate; do not erase until you are ready to hand your paper in
12. Answer all questions; guess unless instructed otherwise
13. Leave time for review

  b. Essay questions
1. Read each question carefully
2. Determine exactly what is wanted. Underline key words or phrases.
3. Decide on outline or paragraph answer
4. Include many different points and elements unless asked to develop any one or two points or elements
5. Show impartiality by giving pros and cons unless directed to select one side only
6. Make and write down any assumptions you find necessary to answer the questions
7. Watch your English, grammar, punctuation and choice of words
8. Time your answers; don't crowd material

8) Answering the essay question

Most essay questions can be answered by framing the specific response around several key words or ideas. Here are a few such key words or ideas:

M's: manpower, materials, methods, money, management
P's: purpose, program, policy, plan, procedure, practice, problems, pitfalls, personnel, public relations

  a. Six basic steps in handling problems:
1. Preliminary plan and background development
2. Collect information, data and facts
3. Analyze and interpret information, data and facts
4. Analyze and develop solutions as well as make recommendations
5. Prepare report and sell recommendations
6. Install recommendations and follow up effectiveness

  b. Pitfalls to avoid
1. *Taking things for granted* – A statement of the situation does not necessarily imply that each of the elements is necessarily true; for example, a complaint may be invalid and biased so that all that can be taken for granted is that a complaint has been registered

2. *Considering only one side of a situation* – Wherever possible, indicate several alternatives and then point out the reasons you selected the best one
3. *Failing to indicate follow up* – Whenever your answer indicates action on your part, make certain that you will take proper follow-up action to see how successful your recommendations, procedures or actions turn out to be
4. *Taking too long in answering any single question* – Remember to time your answers properly

IX. AFTER THE TEST

Scoring procedures differ in detail among civil service jurisdictions although the general principles are the same. Whether the papers are hand-scored or graded by machine we have described, they are nearly always graded by number. That is, the person who marks the paper knows only the number – never the name – of the applicant. Not until all the papers have been graded will they be matched with names. If other tests, such as training and experience or oral interview ratings have been given, scores will be combined. Different parts of the examination usually have different weights. For example, the written test might count 60 percent of the final grade, and a rating of training and experience 40 percent. In many jurisdictions, veterans will have a certain number of points added to their grades.

After the final grade has been determined, the names are placed in grade order and an eligible list is established. There are various methods for resolving ties between those who get the same final grade – probably the most common is to place first the name of the person whose application was received first. Job offers are made from the eligible list in the order the names appear on it. You will be notified of your grade and your rank as soon as all these computations have been made. This will be done as rapidly as possible.

People who are found to meet the requirements in the announcement are called "eligibles." Their names are put on a list of eligible candidates. An eligible's chances of getting a job depend on how high he stands on this list and how fast agencies are filling jobs from the list.

When a job is to be filled from a list of eligibles, the agency asks for the names of people on the list of eligibles for that job. When the civil service commission receives this request, it sends to the agency the names of the three people highest on this list. Or, if the job to be filled has specialized requirements, the office sends the agency the names of the top three persons who meet these requirements from the general list.

The appointing officer makes a choice from among the three people whose names were sent to him. If the selected person accepts the appointment, the names of the others are put back on the list to be considered for future openings.

That is the rule in hiring from all kinds of eligible lists, whether they are for typist, carpenter, chemist, or something else. For every vacancy, the appointing officer has his choice of any one of the top three eligibles on the list. This explains why the person whose name is on top of the list sometimes does not get an appointment when some of the persons lower on the list do. If the appointing officer chooses the second or third eligible, the No. 1 eligible does not get a job at once, but stays on the list until he is appointed or the list is terminated.

X. HOW TO PASS THE INTERVIEW TEST

The examination for which you applied requires an oral interview test. You have already taken the written test and you are now being called for the interview test – the final part of the formal examination.

You may think that it is not possible to prepare for an interview test and that there are no procedures to follow during an interview. Our purpose is to point out some things you can do in advance that will help you and some good rules to follow and pitfalls to avoid while you are being interviewed.

What is an interview supposed to test?

The written examination is designed to test the technical knowledge and competence of the candidate; the oral is designed to evaluate intangible qualities, not readily measured otherwise, and to establish a list showing the relative fitness of each candidate – as measured against his competitors – for the position sought. Scoring is not on the basis of "right" and "wrong," but on a sliding scale of values ranging from "not passable" to "outstanding." As a matter of fact, it is possible to achieve a relatively low score without a single "incorrect" answer because of evident weakness in the qualities being measured.

Occasionally, an examination may consist entirely of an oral test – either an individual or a group oral. In such cases, information is sought concerning the technical knowledges and abilities of the candidate, since there has been no written examination for this purpose. More commonly, however, an oral test is used to supplement a written examination.

Who conducts interviews?

The composition of oral boards varies among different jurisdictions. In nearly all, a representative of the personnel department serves as chairman. One of the members of the board may be a representative of the department in which the candidate would work. In some cases, "outside experts" are used, and, frequently, a businessman or some other representative of the general public is asked to serve. Labor and management or other special groups may be represented. The aim is to secure the services of experts in the appropriate field.

However the board is composed, it is a good idea (and not at all improper or unethical) to ascertain in advance of the interview who the members are and what groups they represent. When you are introduced to them, you will have some idea of their backgrounds and interests, and at least you will not stutter and stammer over their names.

What should be done before the interview?

While knowledge about the board members is useful and takes some of the surprise element out of the interview, there is other preparation which is more substantive. It *is* possible to prepare for an oral interview – in several ways:

1) Keep a copy of your application and review it carefully before the interview

This may be the only document before the oral board, and the starting point of the interview. Know what education and experience you have listed there, and the sequence and dates of all of it. Sometimes the board will ask you to review the highlights of your experience for them; you should not have to hem and haw doing it.

2) Study the class specification and the examination announcement

Usually, the oral board has one or both of these to guide them. The qualities, characteristics or knowledges required by the position sought are stated in these documents. They offer valuable clues as to the nature of the oral interview. For example, if the job involves supervisory responsibilities, the announcement will usually indicate that knowledge of modern supervisory methods and the qualifications of the candidate as a supervisor will be tested. If so, you can expect such questions, frequently in the form of a hypothetical situation which you are expected to solve. NEVER go into an oral without knowledge of the duties and responsibilities of the job you seek.

3) Think through each qualification required

Try to visualize the kind of questions you would ask if you were a board member. How well could you answer them? Try especially to appraise your own knowledge and background in each area, *measured against the job sought*, and identify any areas in which you are weak. Be critical and realistic – do not flatter yourself.

4) Do some general reading in areas in which you feel you may be weak

For example, if the job involves supervision and your past experience has NOT, some general reading in supervisory methods and practices, particularly in the field of human relations, might be useful. Do NOT study agency procedures or detailed manuals. The oral board will be testing your understanding and capacity, not your memory.

5) Get a good night's sleep and watch your general health and mental attitude

You will want a clear head at the interview. Take care of a cold or any other minor ailment, and of course, no hangovers.

What should be done on the day of the interview?

Now comes the day of the interview itself. Give yourself plenty of time to get there. Plan to arrive somewhat ahead of the scheduled time, particularly if your appointment is in the fore part of the day. If a previous candidate fails to appear, the board might be ready for you a bit early. By early afternoon an oral board is almost invariably behind schedule if there are many candidates, and you may have to wait. Take along a book or magazine to read, or your application to review, but leave any extraneous material in the waiting room when you go in for your interview. In any event, relax and compose yourself.

The matter of dress is important. The board is forming impressions about you – from your experience, your manners, your attitude, and your appearance. Give your personal appearance careful attention. Dress your best, but not your flashiest. Choose conservative, appropriate clothing, and be sure it is immaculate. This is a business interview, and your appearance should indicate that you regard it as such. Besides, being well groomed and properly dressed will help boost your confidence.

Sooner or later, someone will call your name and escort you into the interview room. *This is it.* From here on you are on your own. It is too late for any more preparation. But remember, you asked for this opportunity to prove your fitness, and you are here because your request was granted.

What happens when you go in?

The usual sequence of events will be as follows: The clerk (who is often the board stenographer) will introduce you to the chairman of the oral board, who will introduce you to the other members of the board. Acknowledge the introductions before you sit down. Do not be surprised if you find a microphone facing you or a stenotypist sitting by. Oral interviews are usually recorded in the event of an appeal or other review.

Usually the chairman of the board will open the interview by reviewing the highlights of your education and work experience from your application – primarily for the benefit of the other members of the board, as well as to get the material into the record. Do not interrupt or comment unless there is an error or significant misinterpretation; if that is the case, do not hesitate. But do not quibble about insignificant matters. Also, he will usually ask you some question about your education, experience or your present job – partly to get you to start talking and to establish the interviewing "rapport." He may start the actual questioning, or turn it over to one of the other members. Frequently, each member undertakes the questioning on a particular area, one in which he is perhaps most competent, so you can expect each member to participate in the examination. Because time is limited, you may also expect some rather abrupt switches in the direction the questioning takes, so do not be upset by it. Normally, a board member will not pursue a single line of questioning unless he discovers a particular strength or weakness.

After each member has participated, the chairman will usually ask whether any member has any further questions, then will ask you if you have anything you wish to add. Unless you are expecting this question, it may floor you. Worse, it may start you off on an extended, extemporaneous speech. The board is not usually seeking more information. The question is principally to offer you a last opportunity to present further qualifications or to indicate that you have nothing to add. So, if you feel that a significant qualification or characteristic has been overlooked, it is proper to point it out in a sentence or so. Do not compliment the board on the thoroughness of their examination – they have been sketchy, and you know it. If you wish, merely say, "No thank you, I have nothing further to add." This is a point where you can "talk yourself out" of a good impression or fail to present an important bit of information. Remember, *you close the interview yourself.*

The chairman will then say, "That is all, Mr. _____, thank you." Do not be startled; the interview is over, and quicker than you think. Thank him, gather your belongings and take your leave. Save your sigh of relief for the other side of the door.

How to put your best foot forward

Throughout this entire process, you may feel that the board individually and collectively is trying to pierce your defenses, seek out your hidden weaknesses and embarrass and confuse you. Actually, this is not true. They are obliged to make an appraisal of your qualifications for the job you are seeking, and they want to see you in your best light. Remember, they must interview all candidates and a non-cooperative candidate may become a failure in spite of their best efforts to bring out his qualifications. Here are 15 suggestions that will help you:

1) **Be natural – Keep your attitude confident, not cocky**

If you are not confident that you can do the job, do not expect the board to be. Do not apologize for your weaknesses, try to bring out your strong points. The board is interested in a positive, not negative, presentation. Cockiness will antagonize any board member and make him wonder if you are covering up a weakness by a false show of strength.

2) **Get comfortable, but don't lounge or sprawl**

Sit erectly but not stiffly. A careless posture may lead the board to conclude that you are careless in other things, or at least that you are not impressed by the importance of the occasion. Either conclusion is natural, even if incorrect. Do not fuss with your clothing, a pencil or an ashtray. Your hands may occasionally be useful to emphasize a point; do not let them become a point of distraction.

3) **Do not wisecrack or make small talk**

This is a serious situation, and your attitude should show that you consider it as such. Further, the time of the board is limited – they do not want to waste it, and neither should you.

4) Do not exaggerate your experience or abilities

In the first place, from information in the application or other interviews and sources, the board may know more about you than you think. Secondly, you probably will not get away with it. An experienced board is rather adept at spotting such a situation, so do not take the chance.

5) If you know a board member, do not make a point of it, yet do not hide it

Certainly you are not fooling him, and probably not the other members of the board. Do not try to take advantage of your acquaintanceship – it will probably do you little good.

6) Do not dominate the interview

Let the board do that. They will give you the clues – do not assume that you have to do all the talking. Realize that the board has a number of questions to ask you, and do not try to take up all the interview time by showing off your extensive knowledge of the answer to the first one.

7) Be attentive

You only have 20 minutes or so, and you should keep your attention at its sharpest throughout. When a member is addressing a problem or question to you, give him your undivided attention. Address your reply principally to him, but do not exclude the other board members.

8) Do not interrupt

A board member may be stating a problem for you to analyze. He will ask you a question when the time comes. Let him state the problem, and wait for the question.

9) Make sure you understand the question

Do not try to answer until you are sure what the question is. If it is not clear, restate it in your own words or ask the board member to clarify it for you. However, do not haggle about minor elements.

10) Reply promptly but not hastily

A common entry on oral board rating sheets is "candidate responded readily," or "candidate hesitated in replies." Respond as promptly and quickly as you can, but do not jump to a hasty, ill-considered answer.

11) Do not be peremptory in your answers

A brief answer is proper – but do not fire your answer back. That is a losing game from your point of view. The board member can probably ask questions much faster than you can answer them.

12) Do not try to create the answer you think the board member wants

He is interested in what kind of mind you have and how it works – not in playing games. Furthermore, he can usually spot this practice and will actually grade you down on it.

13) Do not switch sides in your reply merely to agree with a board member

Frequently, a member will take a contrary position merely to draw you out and to see if you are willing and able to defend your point of view. Do not start a debate, yet do not surrender a good position. If a position is worth taking, it is worth defending.

14) Do not be afraid to admit an error in judgment if you are shown to be wrong

The board knows that you are forced to reply without any opportunity for careful consideration. Your answer may be demonstrably wrong. If so, admit it and get on with the interview.

15) Do not dwell at length on your present job

The opening question may relate to your present assignment. Answer the question but do not go into an extended discussion. You are being examined for a *new* job, not your present one. As a matter of fact, try to phrase ALL your answers in terms of the job for which you are being examined.

Basis of Rating

Probably you will forget most of these "do's" and "don'ts" when you walk into the oral interview room. Even remembering them all will not ensure you a passing grade. Perhaps you did not have the qualifications in the first place. But remembering them will help you to put your best foot forward, without treading on the toes of the board members.

Rumor and popular opinion to the contrary notwithstanding, an oral board wants you to make the best appearance possible. They know you are under pressure – but they also want to see how you respond to it as a guide to what your reaction would be under the pressures of the job you seek. They will be influenced by the degree of poise you display, the personal traits you show and the manner in which you respond.

ABOUT THIS BOOK

This book contains tests divided into Examination Sections. Go through each test, answering every question in the margin. We have also attached a sample answer sheet at the back of the book that can be removed and used. At the end of each test look at the answer key and check your answers. On the ones you got wrong, look at the right answer choice and learn. Do not fill in the answers first. Do not memorize the questions and answers, but understand the answer and principles involved. On your test, the questions will likely be different from the samples. Questions are changed and new ones added. If you understand these past questions you should have success with any changes that arise. Tests may consist of several types of questions. We have additional books on each subject should more study be advisable or necessary for you. Finally, the more you study, the better prepared you will be. This book is intended to be the last thing you study before you walk into the examination room. Prior study of relevant texts is also recommended. NLC publishes some of these in our Fundamental Series. Knowledge and good sense are important factors in passing your exam. Good luck also helps. So now study this Passbook, absorb the material contained within and take that knowledge into the examination. Then do your best to pass that exam.

EXAMINATION SECTION

EXAMINATION SECTION
TEST 1

DIRECTIONS: Each question or incomplete statement is followed by several suggested answers or completions. Select the one that BEST answers the question or completes the statement. *PRINT THE LETTER OF THE CORRECT ANSWER IN THE SPACE AT THE RIGHT.*

1. A notary public is BEST described as a(n)
   A. amicus curiae
   B. public official
   C. legal counsel
   D. actuary

2. The office of notary public was established by
   A. Ancient Greece
   B. Medieval England
   C. the Roman Empire
   D. Colonial America

3. Newly commissioned notaries public are required to file their oath of office and official signature with the county clerk within ___ days.
   A. 10
   B. 30
   C. 60
   D. 90

4. A county clerk's authentication of a notary's authority is USUALLY obtained when the document
   A. specifies a land conveyance
   B. is to be used in New York City
   C. requires such authentication
   D. is used outside New York State

5. If a notary expects to sign documents outside his county of residence, he may elect to file his oath of office and signature with
   A. other county clerks
   B. the Secretary of State
   C. the State Supreme Court
   D. no one else

6. Which of the following may a non-resident notary do?
   A. Notarize wills
   B. Issue certified copies
   C. Take protests of note
   D. Take depositions

7. If one wishes to sue a non-resident notary public, the summons may be served upon the
   A. county clerk
   B. attorney general
   C. Secretary of State
   D. notary only

8. Which of the following may a notary public do?
   A. Advertise
   B. Execute an acknowledgment of a will
   C. Give legal advice
   D. Draw up a deed

9. A notary who practices law may, besides being removed from office be punished for
   A. slander
   B. libel
   C. felony
   D. criminal contempt

10. The number of notaries public is determined by
    A. the legislature
    B. the civil service commission
    C. the Secretary of State
    D. individual county clerks

11. The jurisdiction of a notary public extends throughout the
    A. United States
    B. state only
    C. county of residence only
    D. city of residence only

12. The MAXIMUM length of term of a notary is
    A. 6 months
    B. 1 year
    C. 2 years
    D. 4 years

13. Every person appointed as a notary public MUST
    A. be a United States citizen
    B. be a resident of the state
    C. have a place of business in the state
    D. be a registered voter

14. The educational requirement for a notary public is
    A. common school education
    B. high school diploma
    C. college degree
    D. none

15. A notary public MUST be at time of application for appointment ____ years old.
    A. 18   B. 20   C. 21   D. 25

16. A candidate for the office of notary public may NOT be appointed if he has been convicted of which of the following?
    A. Drunken driving
    B. Misdemeanor
    C. Possessing burglar's instruments
    D. Traffic offenses

17. The fee for taking an acknowledgment and swearing two witnesses is
    A. 50¢   B. $1.00   C. $6.00   D. $7.50

18. If a person does not file his oath of office within the prescribed time, his appointment is revoked. How may he then become a notary?
    A. Reapplying, paying fee, and passing the examination
    B. Reapplying and paying the fee
    C. Paying the fee
    D. He may not

19. The fee for a county clerk's certificate of official character is
    A. 25¢   B. 50¢   C. $1.00   D. $5.00

20. Which of the following may a notary public NOT do on Sunday?
    A. Take an acknowledgment
    B. Administer an oath
    C. Take an affidavit
    D. Take a deposition

21. Any person who is NOT a notary but who represents himself as such is guilty of 21.___
    A. misdemeanor B. felony C. harassment D. perjury

22. The person named by a court to administer the estate of a man who has died without leaving a will is called the 22.___
    A. executor
    C. administrator
    B. intestate
    D. surrogate

23. The person named in a will to administer the estate of the deceased is called the 23.___
    A. executor
    C. administrator
    B. intestate
    D. surrogate

24. The act of carrying on legal action is called 24.___
    A. heirsuit
    C. protestation
    B. litigation
    D. perjury

25. Which of the following is an ex parte statement? 25.___
    A. Deposition
    C. Affidavit
    B. Acknowledgment
    D. Conveyance

KEY (CORRECT ANSWERS)

1. B
2. C
3. B
4. D
5. A

6. D
7. C
8. B
9. D
10. C

11. B
12. D
13. A
14. A
15. A

16. C
17. C
18. B
19. D
20. D

21. A
22. C
23. A
24. B
25. C

TEST 2

DIRECTIONS: Each question or incomplete statement is followed by several suggested answers or completions. Select the one that BEST answers the question or completes the statement. *PRINT THE LETTER OF THE CORRECT ANSWER IN THE SPACE AT THE RIGHT.*

1. The maker of a deposition is called the
   - A. depositor
   - B. affiant
   - C. attestor
   - D. deponent

2. For an oath to be effective, it MUST be
   - A. oral
   - B. written
   - C. witnessed
   - D. all of the above

3. The equivalent of an oath is a(n)
   - A. attestation
   - B. affirmation
   - C. chattel
   - D. deposition

4. The transfer, surrender, or assignment of any interest in real property is called a(n)
   - A. lien
   - B. mortgage
   - C. sale
   - D. conveyance

5. An agreement between competent parties to do or not to do certain things for legal consideration, whereby each acquires a right to what the other possesses, is a
   - A. consideration
   - B. bill of sale
   - C. contract
   - D. lien

6. An escrow should be revocable by
   - A. the first party
   - B. the escrowee
   - C. either party
   - D. no one

7. A crime punishable by imprisonment in a state prison is a(n)
   - A. perjury
   - B. misdemeanor
   - C. offense
   - D. felony

8. The part of an affidavit where the notary public certifies that it was sworn to before him is the
   - A. lien
   - B. codicil
   - C. jurat
   - D. seal

9. The evidence of a personal debt secured by real property is USUALLY in the form of a
   - A. mortgage
   - B. lien
   - C. lease
   - D. bond

10. An instrument in writing that creates a lien upon real estate as security for the payment of a specified debt is a(n)
    - A. conveyance
    - B. mortgage
    - C. escrow
    - D. lease

11. The one of the following that the state does NOT require the notary to use is the
    - A. signature
    - B. jurat
    - C. venue
    - D. seal

12. The part of the state law which requires that certain contracts MUST be in writing or partially complied with, in order to be enforceable at law, is called the 12.___
    A. contract law   B. common law
    C. proof clause   D. statute of frauds

13. Laws which are passed by legislatures are called 13.___
    A. bills   B. statutes   C. contracts   D. codes

14. If a notary public fails to administer an oath, he is guilty of 14.___
    A. removal from office   B. misdemeanor
    C. felony   D. none of the above

15. If the lessee of a safe deposit box fails to pay rental or does not vacate the box after the prescribed period of time by law, the box may be opened by a notary accompanied by a 15.___
    A. locksmith   B. county clerk
    C. bank guard   D. bank officer

16. The contents of such a safe deposit box shall, after the expiration of ten years from the time of opening of the box, be deemed ____ property. 16.___
    A. lost   B. government   C. destroyed   D. abandoned

17. The one of the following which a notary may NOT do is: 17.___
    A. Take an acknowledgment on a conveyance
    B. Perform marriages
    C. Charge for his services
    D. Administer oaths

18. A person who communicates by telephone or mail in a manner likely to cause annoyance or alarm is guilty of 18.___
    A. felony   B. assault
    C. battery   D. harassment

19. A notary who issues a false certificate with intent to defraud or deceive with knowledge that it contains a false statement or false information is guilty of a class ____ felony. 19.___
    A. B   B. C   C. D   D. E

20. A person guilty of forgery in the second degree is guilty of a class ____ felony. 20.___
    A. B   B. C   C. D   D. E

21. If a notary is convicted of official misconduct, what may his MAXIMUM sentence be? 21.___
    A. 30 days   B. 6 months
    C. 1 year   D. 4 years

22. If a notary asks for and receives more compensation than he is allowed by law, he is subject to indictment. Which of the following charges would he NOT be indicted with? 22.___
    A. Criminal contempt   B. Treble damages
    C. Criminal prosecution   D. Felony

23. The acknowledgment or proof of a conveyance of real property situate may NOT be made before a
    A. real estate broker
    B. justice of the Supreme Court
    C. title examiner
    D. notary public

24. The thing to be known by the notary in taking an acknowledgment is the
    A. facts
    B. identity of the maker is the same as the executor
    C. truth of the acknowledgment
    D. reason

25. What is the fee for administering an oath to a military officer, public official, or public employee?
    A. 25¢
    B. 50¢
    C. $2.00
    D. Nothing

KEY (CORRECT ANSWERS)

1. D	11. D
2. A	12. D
3. B	13. B
4. D	14. B
5. C	15. D
6. D	16. D
7. D	17. B
8. C	18. D
9. D	19. D
10. B	20. C

21. C
22. A
23. A
24. B
25. D

EXAMINATION SECTION
TEST 1

DIRECTIONS: Each question or incomplete statement is followed by several suggested answers or completions. Select the one that BEST answers the question or completes the statement. *PRINT THE LETTER OF THE CORRECT ANSWER IN THE SPACE AT THE RIGHT.*

1. The *primary* duty of a Notary Public is to 1.___
   A. administer oaths, and take proof and acknowledgement of written instruments
   B. attest to the genuineness of any deeds or writings in order to render them available as evidence of the facts therein contained
   C. take acknowledge of or proof of the execution of an instrument by his client in respect to any matter, claim or proceeding
   D. attest to the genuineness of notice, in that one who is entitled to notice of a fact, will thus be bound by acquiring knowledge of it
   E. attest that a person has notice of a fact when he has actual knowledge thereof, or has received a notification thereof from all the facts and circumstances known to him at the time in question

2. How is the fee to which a notary is entitled set? 2.___
   A. Each notary sets his own fee
   B. The fee is determined by agreement
   C. Each notary sets his own fee except in cases where he performs service for a corporation in which he is employed
   D. By law
   E. There is no fee

3. Who appoints and commissions notaries public? The 3.___
   A. Attorney General
   B. Commissioner of General Services
   C. Secretary of State
   D. Solicitor General
   E. Governor

4. The JURAT is 4.___
   A. evidence that the person making the acknowledgment is the individual described in, and who executed the document
   B. evidence of the truth of the matters in relation to which he certifies
   C. evidence that the oath was properly taken before a duly authorized officer
   D. a part of the oath
   E. conclusive evidence of an oath's due administration

5. A notary public who practices any fraud or deceit in the performance of his duties can be convicted of 5.___
   A. misconduct   B. a misdemeanor   C. malpractice
   D. fraud   E. a felony

7

6. All of the following are duties of a notary public EXCEPT:
   A. Attesting to an affirmation
   B. Taking an acknowledgment
   C. Taking a deposition
   D. Administering an oath
   E. Drawing a will

7. In notarial practice, which of the following conditions is MOST important? The deponent
   A. is who he says he is
   B. understands the ramifications of all he is swearing to
   C. is competent
   D. can pay the fee
   E. is known to the notary

8. The place on a notary certificate that gives the location where the notarial act was performed is called the
   A. scilicet
   B. venue
   C. testimonium clause
   D. verification
   E. subscription

9. A notary public may lawfully
   A. execute an acknowledgment to a will
   B. take an acknowledge to a legal instrument in which he has a financial interest
   C. take the acknowledgment of his constituent
   D. take the acknowledgment of a third party
   E. None of the above

10. A notary public is NOT permitted to adminster an oath to
    A. a military officer
    B. a public official
    C. a member of his family
    D. himself
    E. all of the above

11. When an appointee does not file his oath of office within the specified time period
    A. his appointment is revoked
    B. his fee is refunded
    C. he cannot apply for a new appointment for at least six months
    D. he is required to pass another examination for the same appointment
    E. he is guilty of a misdemeanor

12. All persons commissioned as notaries public
    A. must be native born citizens
    B. must have high school diplomas
    C. are commissioned at the discretion of the Secretary of State
    D. must have some legal background
    E. all of the above

13. An ATTESTATION is performed by a   13.___
    A. deponent   B. witness   C. attorney
    D. litigant   E. notary public

14. A notary public CANNOT give legal advice EXCEPT when he   14.___
    A. makes known the fact that he is not an attorney
    B. does not collect a fee
    C. has a law degree
    D. finds it necessary to properly perform his duties as notary
    E. none of the above

15. A JURAT is added to   15.___
    A. a certificate   B. an affidavit
    C. a certificate of authority   D. an attestation
    E. an affirmation

16. A person who receives services from a notary public is properly termed a   16.___
    A. client   B. bearer   C. advocate
    D. constituent   E. customer

17. A person who has failed to reapply for appointment on account of enlistment in the armed forces, must apply for reappointment within _____ after military discharge.   17.___
    A. 30 days   B. 3 months   C. 6 months
    D. 1 year   E. 2 years

18. NO person may be appointed as a notary public who has been convicted of a felony   18.___
    A. in any state or territory of the United States
    B. in the county of jurisdiction
    C. in any county within the state
    D. in the state, if the conviction occurred after the age of 21
    E. in any place in the world

19. Which of the following is a legal impediment to a person being appointed to the office of notary public?   19.___
    A. Illegally using or carrying a pistol
    B. Receiving or having criminal possession of stolen property
    C. Unlawful possession of a habit forming narcotic drug
    D. Unlawful entry of a building
    E. All of the above

20. Which of the following is TRUE of a town official appointed as a notary public?   20.___
    A. The notary may NOT retain the fees collected
    B. The expense of his appointment is NOT a proper town charge
    C. Only non-elected officials may be appointed notaries
    D. Fees collected for notarial services performed for the general public must be split with the town
    E. The notary may NOT waive collection of any fee

21. The making of a useless certificate and the collection of a fee therefor after receipt of notice that such practices must be discontinued, justifies a finding of
    A. misfeasance
    B. malpractice
    C. insubordination
    D. liability
    E. misconduct

22. An affiant who swears falsely may be prosecuted for
    A. counterfeiting
    B. fraud
    C. perjury
    D. forgery
    E. misrepresentation

23. The signature of the notary public is to be made in
    A. blue ink
    B. black ink
    C. blue or black ink
    D. any color ink
    E. any color ink or by any writing instrument as long as the signature is legible

24. A person may become a notary public if his appointment was revoked by failure to file within the specified period of time by
    A. reapplying
    B. paying a fee
    C. reapplying and paying a fee
    D. reapplying and passing the qualifying exam
    E. reapplying, paying a fee and passing the qualifying exam

25. The act of admitting or recognizing the existence of a signed agreement as evidence of one's intention that the agreement be binding and in full force is known as a(n)
    A. acceptance
    B. acknowledgment
    C. notarial act
    D. transaction
    E. certification

KEY (CORRECT ANSWERS)

1. A	6. E	11. A	16. D	21. E
2. D	7. A	12. C	17. D	22. C
3. C	8. B	13. B	18. A	23. B
4. C	9. C	14. E	19. E	24. C
5. B	10. D	15. B	20. B	25. B

TEST 2

DIRECTIONS: Each question or incomplete statement is followed by several suggested answers or completions. Select the one that BEST answers the question or completes the statement. *PRINT THE LETTER OF THE CORRECT ANSWER IN THE SPACE AT THE RIGHT.*

1. A document used as testimony in a court proceeding is called a(n) 1.___
   - A. instrument
   - B. writ
   - C. deposition
   - D. subpoena
   - E. testament

2. A duly qualified notary public is deemed capable of performing notarial acts in accordance with the 2.___
   - A. wishes of the Secretary of State
   - B. wishes of the Governor
   - C. dictates of his conscience
   - D. needs of society
   - E. law

3. A misdemeanor is a(n) 3.___
   - A. intentionally wrongful or improper act
   - B. lesser crime than a felony
   - C. unlawful performance of an act
   - D. minor felony
   - E. violation

4. It is incumbent on the notary to scrutinize each document presented in order to 4.___
   - A. insure it is in the form prescribed by law
   - B. determine if an oath is required
   - C. see that the person who executed the instrument has not signed his name without the presence of the notary
   - D. determine the exact nature of his duty with regard to the document
   - E. determine if the venue falls within his jurisdiction

5. Notaries must administer oaths in the manner and form prescribed by the 5.___
   - A. Real Property Law
   - B. Judiciary Law
   - C. Public Officers Law
   - D. Executive Law
   - E. Civil Practice Law and Rules

6. A notary who was appointed under the name of Robert T. Jones may sign as 6.___
   - A. Robert T. Jones
   - B. Robt. T. Jones
   - C. R. Jones
   - D. R.T. Jones
   - E. all of the above

7. The signature and seal of a county clerk upon a certificate of the official character of a notary public may be 7.___
   - A. printed
   - B. photographed
   - C. engraved
   - D. a facsimile
   - E. all of the above

8. When is it NOT illegal to take an acknowledgment over the telephone?
   A. It is always illegal
   B. When the notary has satisfactory evidence that the person making it is the person described
   C. When no jurat is required
   D. When venue is not an issue
   E. When the words: "On this ___ day of ___, 20___, before me came..." are excluded

9. Under what circumstance is the notary permitted to receive a greater fee for a service than normally allowed by law?
   A. When it is not solicited or in any way demanded
   B. When travel expenses are incurred
   C. When the affidavits exceed one printed page
   D. When personal inconvenience or extenuating circumstances demand it
   E. Under no circumstance

10. A notary who is a stockholder of a corporation may
    A. NOT protest for the non-acceptance of negotiable instruments owned by the corporation
    B. NOT protest for the non-payment of negotiable instruments owned by that corporation
    C. protest for the non-acceptance and non-payment of negotiable instruments owned or held for collection by that corporation
    D. protest for the non-acceptance and non-payment of negotiable instruments held for collection by that corporation
    E. protest only for non-acceptance of negotiable instruments owned or held for collection by that corporation

11. The subscribing witness to any instrument verified or acknowledged before a notary public is the
    A. notary public   B. constituent   C. affiant
    D. maker   E. county clerk

12. Which of the following may preclude a person from becoming a notary public? If he
    A. holds another public office
    B. is a commissioned military officer
    C. is a retired public employee
    D. is a minor
    E. all of the above

13. The powers of notaries public are defined by
    A. the Secretary of State   B. courts of record
    C. statute   D. tradition
    E. convention

14. A notary may take a deposition if he is NOT
    A. an attorney for a party or prospective party seeking the examination
    B. the employee of an attorney for the party seeking the examination
    C. a person with an interest
    D. all of the above
    E. none of the above

15. A notary who is a member of the state bar may take the affidavit of his client in respect to any matters when it is taken
    A. prior to a pending cause
    B. with the permission of the court of record
    C. before the suit commences
    D. in the discretion of the Secretary of State
    E. in his discretion

16. Any person WITHOUT an appointment who conveys the impression that he is a notary public may be prosecuted for
    A. misconduct   B. a misdemeanor   C. perjury.
    D. a felony   E. forgery

17. An appointee as a period of ____ to file an oath of office with the county clerk.
    A. 10 days   B. 15 days   C. 30 days
    D. 3 months   E. 6 months

18. Certificates of acknowledgment or proof are NOT entitled to be read in evidence or recorded in this state if they are made in a foreign country other than
    A. United Kingdom B. Canada   C. Guam
    D. Mexico   E. in an English speaking nation

19. To indicate genuineness by signing as a witness, the notary public _____ the instrument.
    A. authenticates   B. endorses   C. attests
    D. certifies   E. affirms

20. A notary public who knowingly makes a false certificate may be prosecuted for
    A. malfeasance   B. forgery   C. misconduct
    D. a misdemeanor   E. malpractice

21. The fee for the certification of a notarial signature by a county clerk is
    A. $.25   B. $.50   C. $.75
    D. $1.00   E. $3.00

22. A certificate of official character is issued when a notary wants to practice in other
    A. counties   B. countries   C. cities
    D. states   E. all of the above

23. An attorney would be excluded from the office of, notary public if he is
    A. a resident but not a member of the bar
    B. a non-resident and not admitted to practice in the courts of record of this state
    C. admitted to practice in the courts of record of this state and moves out of state
    D. a non-resident only maintaining an office within this state
    E. none of the above

24. A felony in another jurisdiction, for purpose of disqualification from the office of notary public, depends on all the following EXCEPT
    A. whether executive pardon was received
    B. the exact nature of the crime
    C. the statute upon which the conviction is based
    D. whether the criminal offense is cognizable as a crime in this state
    E. if reciprocity exists

25. What is the fee for affixing a notarial seal to a protest?
    A. Nothing   B. $ .10   C. $ .25
    D. $ .50   E. $ .75

KEY (CORRECT ANSWERS)

1. C	6. A	11. A	16. B	21. E
2. E	7. E	12. D	17. C	22. A
3. B	8. A	13. C	18. B	23. B
4. D	9. E	14. E	19. C	24. E
5. E	10. C	15. E	20. B	25. E

EXAMINATION SECTION
TEST 1

DIRECTIONS: Each question or incomplete statement is followed by several suggested answers or completions. Select the one that BEST answers the question or completes the statement. *PRINT THE LETTER OF THE CORRECT ANSWER IN THE SPACE AT THE RIGHT.*

1. Within what boundaries do the notary's acts receive official credence?
    A. the country in which he serves
    B. the geographic area in which he serves
    C. the state in which he serves
    D. the territorial jurisdiction of the country he serves
    E. the country in which he serves and in all others in which they are used as instruments of evidence

2. In the rural districts of the state, notaries public prepare
    A. leases
    B. bills of sale
    C. chattel mortgages
    D. all of the above
    E. none of the above

3. The qualifying requirements of notaries public are waived in the case of
    A. attorneys
    B. real estate brokers
    C. state officials
    D. county officials
    E. all of the above

4. What is the application fee?
    A. $20.00
    B. $30.00
    C. $40.00
    D. $50.00
    E. $60.00

5. The making of a false jurat by an attorney while acting as a notary public *usually* justifies
    A. a reprimand
    B. his removal
    C. his suspension
    D. censure
    E. disciplinary proceedings leading to disbarment

6. What term has the same meaning as DEPONENT?
    A. bearer
    B. attesting witness
    C. jurat
    D. litigant
    E. affiant

7. A notary public may give legal advice when
    A. it does not involve a criminal action
    B. it does not involve a civil action
    C. it involves real estate
    D. the notary is admitted to practice within the state
    E. none of the above

8. Who signs the JURAT? The
    A. constituent
    B. notary public
    C. county clerk
    D. attorney of record
    E. constituent and the notary

9. The number of notaries public is determined by the 9.___
   A. Secretary of State's judgment
   B. Governor's judgment
   C. number and size of the counties
   D. state population
   E. number of applicants

10. Of the following, which would be more likely to take an oath rather than an affirmation? A(n) 10.___
    A. atheist
    B. member of a religious order
    C. attorney admitted to the bar
    D. person swearing to a legal instrument
    E. notary public

11. The county clerk reports the name and date of the qualification of each notary public and those whose appointment was revoked on 11.___
    A. the last day of each week
    B. the first day of each week
    C. or before the tenth day of each month
    D. or before the last day of each month
    E. March 30th of each year

12. The person who takes the oath to a written instrument is called the 12.___
    A. constituent   B. claimant   C. litigant
    D. affiant   E. testator

13. When should the notary advise the person coming before him as to the law concerning the papers presented for certification? 13.___
    A. Before the oath
    B. After the oath
    C. Before signing his official signature
    D. As soon as possible
    E. None of the above

14. During the time he is available as a notary, a notary public may engage in another business 14.___
    A. at all times
    B. when he sees fit
    C. sometimes
    D. never
    E. only under certain circumstances as specified in the Public Officers Law

15. The license fees charged an applicant for the office of notary public depend on and are determined by the 15.___
    A. Secretary of State
    B. volume of fees collected by the notary during his previous appointment
    C. population of the county of his residence
    D. area size of the county of his residence
    E. notary's term of office

16. An applicant for appointment as notary public shall be in form and set forth such matters as the ____ shall prescribe.
    A. law
    B. governor and senate
    C. secretary of state
    D. county clerk
    E. applicant

17. A member of the armed forces may have the qualifying requirements waived is his discharge was
    A. honorable *only*
    B. under conditions other than honorable
    C. general *only*
    D. administrative *only*
    E. under conditions other than dishonorable

18. The power to suspend or remove a notary from office rests with
    A. the governor
    B. the secretary of state
    C. the attorney general
    D. a court of law
    E. the senate

19. Necessary forms for application for appointment as a notary public are supplied by offices in
    A. Albany
    B. New York City
    C. Buffalo
    D. Poughkeepsie
    E. any major city throughout the state

20. Which of the following is not reported to the Secretary of State? The
    A. name of each notary public qualifying
    B. date of qualification
    C. fee collected for qualification
    D. name of each notary public whose appointment was revoked
    E. fee forfeited for failure to qualify

21. A notary who makes a useless certificate and collects a fee after receiving notice to discontinue such practice warrants
    A. a fine
    B. his suspension from office
    C. an official reprimand
    D. forfeiture of the fee
    E. his removal from office

22. Failure to affix the official county clerk number to an instrument,
    A. invalidates the oath
    B. invalidates the instrument
    C. does NOT invalidate the instrument
    D. releases a false swearer from prosecution
    E. constitutes misconduct

23. The notary adds the name of any county in which his certificate of official character is filed
    A. whenever it is required
    B. when it is filed in a county or counties within the city of New York
    C. when it is requested he do so by the affiant
    D. when he is not an attorney with a practice of law within this state
    E. at no time

24. When a notary public has qualified in the office of the clerk in a county or counties within the City of New York, each instrument must have the
    A. words: "Notary Public, City of New York"
    B. name of the county or counties
    C. name of other county or counties of qualification
    D. official number or numbers given to him by the clerk
    E. embossment of his official seal

25. A notary must know
    A. how to prepare a legal document
    B. state law
    C. the acts which constitute the practice of law
    D. the acts which constitute the practice of a notary public *only*
    E. which acts constitute the practice of law and which acts constitute the practice of a notary public

KEY (CORRECT ANSWERS)

1. E	6. E	11. C	16. C	21. E
2. E	7. D	12. D	17. E	22. C
3. A	8. B	13. E	18. B	23. A
4. E	9. A	14. A	19. A	24. D
5. C	10. B	15. C	20. C	25. E

TEST 2

DIRECTIONS: Each question or incomplete statement is followed by several suggested answers or completions. Select the one that BEST answers the question or completes the statement. *PRINT THE LETTER OF THE CORRECT ANSWER IN THE SPACE AT THE RIGHT.*

1. A document may also be called a(n) 1.___
   - A. affidavit
   - B. declaration
   - C. transcript
   - D. instrument
   - E. certificate

2. A felony is a(n) 2.___
   - A. indictment
   - B. violation of the law
   - C. crime more serious than a misdemeanor
   - D. tort
   - E. crime more serious than malfeasance

3. A notary _____ oaths. 3.___
   - A. gives
   - B. takes
   - C. solemnizes
   - D. ratifies
   - E. records

4. A justice of the peace may 4.___
   - A. not take an acknowledgment
   - B. take an acknowledgment only if he signs on the line above the words "notary public"
   - C. take an acknowledgment if he signs on the line provided and crosses out the words "notary public," adding a description of his office
   - D. take an acknowledgment if he signs on the line provided and crosses out the words "notary public"
   - E. take an acknowledgment if he signs in another place besides that reserved for notaries and adds a description of his office under the signature

5. An affidavit differs from a deposition in that an affidavit is 5.___
   - A. abstract
   - B. an ex parte statement
   - C. a res gestae
   - D. not res judicata
   - E. a quasi deposition

6. A notary can take an acknowledgment of a paper which is executed entirely in blank 6.___
   - A. at all times
   - B. at his discretion
   - C. under certain specified circumstances or conditions
   - D. only when the constituent is a fellow notary
   - E. at no time

7. A notary public may 7.___
   - A. solemnize marriages
   - B. not take the acknowledgment of parties and witnesses to a written contract of marriage
   - C. not take depositions to be used in a court proceeding
   - D. issue certified copies
   - E. none of the above

8. A notary's application fee is refundable when the applicant

   A. fails to qualify
   B. fails to qualify within a specified period of time
   C. loses his eligibility
   D. fails to qualify by reason of his induction into the armed forces
   E. under no circumstance

9. A notary fails in his duty with regard to affidavits if he does NOT

   A. certify the execution of the document
   B. certify the identity of the affiant
   C. administer an oath
   D. witness the execution of the document
   E. personally know the person swearing

10. The notary certifies to the taking of the acknowledgment when he

    A. signs his official signature
    B. stamps his rubber stamp
    C. uses his official seal
    D. administers the oath
    E. enters it in his notary's register

11. A notary may NOT take the acknowledgment of a corporation if he

    A. is a stockholder
    B. is an officer
    C. is a party individually executing the instrument
    D. individually or as a representative of the corporation executes the instrument
    E. all of the above

12. When a notary changes his place of residence from one county to another he must notify

    A. only the Secretary of State
    B. the Secretary of State and the county clerk of the new residence
    C. the Secretary of State and the county clerk of the old residence
    D. both county clerks
    E. neither county clerk nor the Secretary of State

13. The cost of securing a commission as notary public for a city veteran's service officer is paid by the

    A. veteran's administration
    B. city
    C. applicant
    D. state
    E. fee is waived

14. A notary's signature to an acknowledgment is authenticated by
    A. the county clerk
    B. the secretary of state
    C. a third person with knowledge of the notary's signature
    D. the maker of the acknowledgment
    E. the notary public

15. Power of Attorney
    A. allows a person to act as attorney for another
    B. is the right of every person admitted to the bar
    C. allows a parent or guardian to act in behalf of a child
    D. allows a person to act in behalf of another
    E. allows a notary to act in behalf of an attorney

16. The making of a false jurat by an attorney while acting as a notary does NOT warrant
    A. imprisonment
    B. disbarment
    C. revoking his notarial license
    D. a fine and/or warning
    E. a reprimand

17. Of the following, it is CORRECT to state that
    A. defects in connection with a notary's statement as to authority cannot be corrected
    B. defects in connection with a notary's statement as to authority are jurisdictional and will invalidate his act
    C. failure to comply with statutory provisions will not validate the acts of a notary
    D. failure to comply with statutory provisions will invalidate the acts of a notary
    E. it is the responsibility of those who use a notary to investigate the notary's right to exercise the functions of the office

18. A notary public can delegate his official authority to
    A. his attorney
    B. an attorney with offices in the same building and who is well known to the notary
    C. his clerk
    D. a third person
    E. none of the above

19. What words may an attorney duly licensed in New York substitute for the words "notary public"?
    A. Attorney-notary
    B. Attorney
    C. Counsellor at law
    D. Attorney and counsellor at law
    E. All of the above

20. A signed statement, duly sworn to by the maker before a notary public is called a(n)
    A. notarization   B. acceptance   C. affidavit
    D. acknowledgment   E. deposition

21. The acknowledgment or proof of a conveyance of real property situate in this state may be made in foreign countries before a notary public
    A. acting within his territorial jurisdiction
    B. appointed to take such without this state
    C. residing within the country where such is taken
    D. specially authorized for such purpose
    E. authorized by the laws of the country where such is taken

22. A jurat does NOT have to include
    A. an official seal
    B. the name of the county he originally qualified in
    C. the date upon which his commission expires
    D. the words: "notary public, state of New York"
    E. none of the above

23. The notary's term of office is
    A. 1 year   B. 2 years   C. 4 years
    D. 10 years   E. variable

24. Which of the following is required for a nonresident to serve as a notary public in this state?
    A. Phone listing in a New York directory
    B. Place of business in New York
    C. Business affiliation with a New York resident
    D. Appointment of a county clerk as person upon whom process can be served on his behalf
    E. Proof of need for appointment

25. A person who was convicted of vagrance or prostitution can serve as a notary public if
    A. the conviction occurred before the age of 18
    B. the conviction occurred before the age of 21
    C. a certificate of good conduct from the parole board removes the disability
    D. the conviction occurred out of state
    E. may not serve

KEY (CORRECT ANSWERS)

1. D	6. E	11. D	16. A	21. A
2. C	7. B	12. E	17. C	22. A
3. A	8. E	13. C	18. E	23. C
4. C	9. C	14. A	19. D	24. B
5. B	10. A	15. D	20. C	25. C

EXAMINATION SECTION
TEST 1

DIRECTIONS: Each question or incomplete statement is followed by several suggested answers or completions. Select the one that BEST answers the question or completes the statement. *PRINT THE LETTER OF THE CORRECT ANSWER IN THE SPACE AT THE RIGHT.*

1. Which of the following statements concerning notarial practice is CORRECT? 1.____
   A. A notary public cannot hold another public office
   B. A retired public employee serves with suspension of pension and annuity benefits
   C. A notary public is prohibited from accepting privileges or favors from corporations
   D. A married woman may not sign using her maiden name even if she married during the course of her term
   E. A Catholic sister is not permitted to sign using her religious name

2. How long must a notary reside in the state preceeding his appointment? 2.____
   A. 6 months   B. 1 year
   C. 2 years   D. 3 years
   E. 5 years

3. A notarization MUST include 3.____
   A. indentations made from the notary's official seal embosser
   B. date upon which the notary's commission began
   C. the notary's official state address
   D. the name of the county where the notary's act took place
   E. the date upon which the notary's commission expires

4. A Catholic sister appointed as a notary public named Jane Smith who wants to sign with her Catholic sister name should sign as 4.____
   A. Sister Mary Joseph
   B. Jane (Sister Mary Joseph) Smith
   C. Jane Smith
   D. Jane Smith (Sister Mary Joseph)
   E. Sister Jane Smith

5. A notary public vacates his office when he 5.____
   A. changes his residence from one county to another within the state
   B. changes his residence from one county within the state to another county outside it while maintaining an office within the state
   C. is a nonresident moving his office from one county to another within the state
   D. is a nonresident moving his office from one county within the state to another outside it
   E. all of the above

6. When an attorney performs an act of notarization, the fee is 6.____
   A. waived   B. set by law
   C. determined by his law office   D. absorbed in the legal fee
   E. set by the Bar Association

7. Which of the following need NOT make a solemn pledge or statement when asked to do so by the notary? A(n)

   A. person known to the notary
   B. member of a religious order
   C. attorney admitted to the bar
   D. atheist
   E. none of the above

8. The fee for adminstering an oath in connection with an affidavit is

   A. $.25
   B. $2.00
   C. $3.00
   D. $5.00
   E. $10.00

9. When the notary public demands acceptance or payment of promissory notes, which results in nonacceptance or nonpayment, he may

   A. issue an adjudication
   B. issue a bill of exchange
   C. issue a claim
   D. petition
   E. issue a notice of protest

10. The fee for the certification of a notarial signature is

    A. $.25
    B. $3.00
    C. $5.00
    D. $10.00
    E. $20.00

11. All persons commissioned as notaries public need NOT

    A. have a residence or office in New York State
    B. have the equivalent of a common school education
    C. pass a qualifying exam
    D. pay certain fees to the county clerk
    E. be persons of good character

12. The expiration date of the term of office for a notary whose appointment took effect on June 12, 2002 is

    A. June 12, 2004
    B. June 12, 2006
    C. March 30, 2005
    D. March 30, 2006
    E. March 31, 2005

13. Which of the following is *acceptable* for a woman who chooses to use her married name during the term her appointment was made in her maiden name?

    A. Mrs. John Smith
    B. Jane Jones
    C. Mrs. John Smith (Jane Jones)
    D. Jane Jones-Smith
    E. Jane Jones (Jane Smith)

14. A person appointed as a notary public must be a citizen
    A. at the time of his appointment
    B. for 30 days prior to his appointment
    C. for 6 months prior to his appointment
    D. for 1 year prior to his appointment
    E. by birth

15. Qualifying requirements may be *waived* if the person applies for reappointment within ____ of the expiration of his term.
    A. 10 days
    B. 30 days
    C. 3 months
    D. 6 months
    E. 1 year

16. When an employee serves as a notary public as a convenience to the county, the fee is
    A. paid by the employee
    B. paid by the county
    C. split between the county and the employee
    D. paid by the state
    E. waived by the county clerk

17. The fee paid by a *foreign* notary MUST be
    A. paid to the foreign notary's consulate
    B. split with the foreign notary's consulate
    C. paid to the state treasury
    D. paid to the secretary of state
    E. paid to the secretary of state of the country

18. The MAXIMUM fee an attorney shall receive for the protest for nonpayment of any note is
    A. $.10
    B. $.25
    C. $.50
    D. $.75
    E. $1.00

19. When a certificate of acknowledgment or proof is made by a notary public in a foreign country, it is NOT entitled tobe read in evidence or recorded in this state *unless*
    A. the person signing the agreement is a citizen
    B. the person signing the agreement is a resident of this state
    C. such certificate is authenticated
    D. such certificate is certified
    E. such certificate is countersigned

20. When a notary *fails* to comply with the provisions governing his authority to act,
    A. the official act is not legally binding
    B. the official act is invalid
    C. the official act is falsified
    D. no fee can be collected
    E. no official act is held invalid

21. The acknowledgment or proof of real property situate in this state may be made by a notary
    A. at any place within the state
    B. within the district he is authorized to perform official duties
    C. within the county he is authorized to perform official duties
    D. within the county where the real property is situated
    E. if it is annexed with a certificate of acknowledgment by a commissioner of deeds

22. The LONGEST term a notary may serve is
    A. 1 year   B. 2 years   C. 4 years
    D. 10 years E. unlimited

23. The notary's signature
    A. should be written in his own hand
    B. ban be written by a designated person
    C. should be stamped on each notarial certificate
    D. should itself be notarized
    E. should be illegible to combat forgery

24. To NOTARIZE means to
    A. swear to the truth
    B. certify
    C. sign a written statement
    D. acknowledge the existence of an agreement
    E. perform a notarial act

25. If a notary prepares and takes the oath of an affiant to a statement he knows to be FALSE, he will be
    A. charged with perjury
    B. suspended
    C. removed from office
    D. fined
    E. prosecuted

KEY (CORRECT ANSWERS)

1. C	6. B	11. C	16. A	21. A
2. B	7. E	12. B	17. D	22. C
3. E	8. B	13. E	18. D	23. A
4. A	9. E	14. A	19. C	24. E
5. D	10. B	15. D	20. E	25. C

TEST 2

DIRECTIONS: Each question or incomplete statement is followed by several suggested answers or completions. Select the one that BEST answers the question or completes the statement. *PRINT THE LETTER OF THE CORRECT ANSWER IN THE SPACE AT THE RIGHT.*

1. A notary's general authority is defined in the 1.___
   A. Real Property Law
   B. Judiciary Law
   C. Public Officers Law
   D. Executive Law
   E. Civil Practice Law and Rules

2. A notary is entitled to a fee for administering the oath of office to a(n) 2.___
   A. military officer
   B. inspector of election
   C. clerk of the poll
   D. public official
   E. none of the above

3. The fee for reappointment is 3.___
   A. nothing
   B. $1.00
   C. $5.00
   D. $20.00
   E. $25.00

4. Which of the following statements concerning the taking of oaths is NOT true? The 4.___
   A. person must swear in the notary's presence
   B. notary must conscientiously take upon himself the obligation of the oath
   C. person must swear that what he states is true
   D. person does not necessarily have to swear before God
   E. None of the above

5. A notary may NOT take the acknowledgment or proof of any party to a written instrument executed by a corporation in which he is a 5.___
   A. stockholder   B. director   C. officer
   D. all of the above   E. none of the above

6. A notary may NOT protest any negotiable instrument owned by a corporation if he is 6.___
   A. a stockholder of that corporation
   B. an officer Of that corporation
   C. an employee of that corporation
   D. individually, a party to such instrument
   E. hone of the above

7. The act of taking and certifying an acknowledgment by a notary is ____ in character. 7.___
   A. judicial
   B. ministerial
   C. legal
   D. constitutional
   E. political

27

8. A notary duly appointed for one county may NOT have his certificate filed in another county if he
   A. refuses to appear personally before the clerk of the other county
   B. does NOT comply with the law relating to the filing of his certificate in the other county
   C. does NOT file within the prescribed period of time
   D. all of the above
   E. hone of the above

9. A notary is NOT authorized to pass upon the competency of a person under the age of _____ years.
   A. 3
   B. 7
   C. 12
   D. 18
   E. 21

10. State courts regard a notary's violation of duty as
    A. serious professional misconduct
    B. intentional misrepresentation
    C. malpractice
    D. malfeasance
    E. wilful wrongdoing

11. Which of the following declarations is accurate regarding the validity of acts of notaries?
    A. A Validation Act declares the validity of acts of notaries public
    B. A Validation Act relieves a notary from criminal liability
    C. A Validation Act relieves a notary from civil liability
    D. Executive Law declares the validity of acts of notaries public
    E. A Validation Act enlarges the actual authority of notaries public

12. A notary CANNOT act in any case in which he has a
    A. financial interest
    B. personal interest
    C. professional interest
    D. business interest
    E. all of the above

13. A notary employed by a bank may divide his fees with the bank
    A. at all times
    B. when he sees fit
    C. sometimes
    D. never
    E. only when they are collected on bank time

14. The authority which notifies each person so appointed to qualify for the commission is the
    A. Secretary of State
    B. County clerk of the county in which appointee resides
    C. County clerk of the county in which appointee qualified
    D. Governor
    E. Board of Examiners

3 (#2)

15. Certification by a notary public that the person named, that appeared before him, and acknowledged to him, that a written release has been executed when neither appearance or signature occurred, constitutes
    A. a felony
    B. a misdemeanor
    C. perjury
    D. malpractice
    E. misconduct

16. An understanding between two or more people is called a(n)
    A. declaration
    B. obligation
    C. liability
    D. contract
    E. agreement

17. Besides a notary, which of the following may take an oath within the area of his authority? A
    A. town official
    B. designated third person
    C. real estate broker
    D. banker
    E. Justice of the peace

18. A justice of the peace and a notary public CANNOT BOTH
    A. perform marriages
    B. take oaths
    C. take acknowledgments
    D. take affadavits
    E. take depositions

19. Taking an affidavit differs from taking an acknowledgment in that
    A. it involves the administration of an oath
    B. it involves certification as to the identity and execution of the document
    C. the identity of the person appearing must be established
    D. the person's appearance must be voluntary
    E. there is NO difference

20. The use of seals by notaries is required by law
    A. at all times
    B. sometimes
    C. at no time
    D. when use is requested
    E. rarely

21. At the time application for appointment is filed, a person MUST be _____ years old.
    A. 16
    B. 17
    C. 18
    D. 21
    E. 25

22. A notary may NOT take proof of a written instrument by or to a corporation if he
    A. is an employee of the corporation
    B. is a stockholder of the corporation
    C. executes the instrument as an individual or representative of the corporation
    D. executes the instrument as a representative of the corporation
    E. none of the above

23. VERIFICATION means
    A. a certified copy
    B. a certificate of acknowledgment
    C. an oath administered by an official to an affiant
    D. a notarization
    E. all of the above

24. A notary is authorized to take a deposition
    A. *only* in the county of jurisdiction
    B. *only* in counties where his certificate is filed
    C. *only* within the state
    D. in any state or place of United States sovereignty
    E. in any state or country where laws of nations are not violated

25. A notarial certificate founded upon a presentment and demand, is void, where the note was NOT presented for payment by the
    A. endorser
    B. notary clerk
    C. notary public
    D. endorsee
    E. county clerk

KEY (CORRECT ANSWERS)

1. D	6. D	11. D	16. E	21. C
2. E	7. B	12. A	17. E	22. C
3. D	8. B	13. D	18. A	23. E
4. B	9. B	14. B	19. A	24. C
5. E	10. A	15. B	20. C	25. C

EXAMINATION SECTION
TEST 1

DIRECTIONS: Each question or incomplete statement is followed by several suggested answers or completions. Select the one that BEST answers the question or completes the statement. *PRINT THE LETTER OF THE CORRECT ANSWER IN THE SPACE AT THE RIGHT.*

1. A notary is considered a
   A. public officer
   B. state officer
   C. judicial officer
   D. magistrate
   E. all of the above

   1.___

2. Which of the following needs written permission from a higher authority in order to hold the office of notary public?
   A. Commissioner of elections
   B. Member of state liquor authority
   C. Custodian of voting machines
   D. Member of the legislature
   E. Town officer

   2.___

3. All of the following are requirements of notaries public EXCEPT:
   A. Applicant has not been convicted of a felony
   B. Applicant has the equivalent of a common school education
   C. Applicant is a citizen of the United States
   D. Applicant's residence and place of employment are within the state
   E. Applicant is familiar with duties and responsibilities of a notary

   3.___

4. A notary is authorized by the Executive Law to do all of the following EXCEPT:
   A. administer oaths and affirmations
   B. take affidavits and depositions
   C. receive and certify acknowledgments, powers of attorney and other instruments in writing
   D. take an affidavit to be used as the basis for a warrant of arrest
   E. demand payment of promissory notes and obligations in writing

   4.___

5. A jurat is *false* when
   A. nothing was sworn to and no oath was administered
   B. it fails to state the jurisdiction of the officer
   C. it is not signed by the notary who took the oath
   D. a notary fails to comply with statutory provisions
   E. there are defects in connection with the notary's statement

   5.___

6. A notary public can waive his fee when
   A. the person coming before him is unable to pay
   B. the act of notarization is for a bank in which he is an employee
   C. the act of notarization is for the county in which he is an employee
   D. the act of notarization involves legal advice
   E. he voluntarily choses to do so

   6.___

7. The fee for the administration of the oath commissioning a notary public is
   A. $.25   B. $3.00   C. $5.00   D. $10.00   E. $20.00

8. A notary public can execute a certificate by
   A. having the person appear before him
   B. telephone, if he recognizes the person's voice
   C. mail, if the person is known to him
   D. having the blood relative of the person appear before him
   E. all of the above

9. A notary may give legal advice if he
   A. shares office space with an attorney
   B. has a business connection with an attorney whose office is not necessarily in the same building as his
   C. has the Secretary of State's authorization
   D. has completed the requirements of a law degree
   E. none of the above

10. A notary public may begin practicing as soon as
    A. he is appointed
    B. he passes the examination
    C. he has filed his autograph signature with the county clerk
    D. he has filed a certificate of his official character with the county clerk
    E. his oath of office is duly executed together with his official signature

11. An affirmation differs from an oath in that
    A. false statements made thereon are not considered perjury
    B. it is not a solemn statement
    C. it is not as binding
    D. it contains no reference to a Supreme Being
    E. there is no difference

12. The sum collected for each certificate of official character issued is
    A. $.25   B. $1.00   C. $3.00
    D. $5.00   E. $10.00

13. Which of the following would disqualify an applicant from appointment as a notary public?
    A. Malfeasance
    B. Misconduct
    C. Conviction of a misdemeanor
    D. Conviction of a felony
    E. All of the above

14. Under what condition can a notary public provide blank forms with his jurat signed at the bottom? When the form is

    A. from a person of integrity known to the notary
    B. from a person the notary has previously performed similar services for and found no evidence of misuse
    C. from a public official whose office may require service at a time the notary is unavailable
    D. a legal document customarily used by an attorney known to the notary
    E. under no circumstances

15. By signing his official signature to the document, the notary _____ to the taking of the acknowledgment.

    A. certifies   B. agrees   C. swears
    D. grants   E. admits

16. The notary's term of office is determined by

    A. the date of his commission
    B. the date he passes the exam
    C. his birthdate
    D. the county in which he serves
    E. his test score

17. Of the following, who must be familiar with the practice of a notary public?

    A. notaries
    B. otaries who are not attorneys
    C. constituents
    D. affiants
    E. process servers

18. The jurisdiction of a notary public is co-extensive with the boundaries

    A. set by the Secretary of State
    B. of the county of residence
    C. of the state
    D. of the country
    E. of county of counties of jurisdiction

19. A nonresident notary public should appoint _____ as the person upon whom process can be served on his behalf.

    A. an attorney whose practice of law is within the state
    B. a resident notary public
    C. a resident of good moral character
    D. the county clerk
    E. the Secretary of State

20. If a notary public applies for a reappointment *before* the expiration of his term

    A. he is excused from the qualifying exam
    B. all fees are waived
    C. qualifying requirements may be waived
    D. the waiting period may be waived
    E. none of the above

21. A notary who is the subject of removal proceedings must have
    A. the representation of counsel
    B. notification within 30 days
    C. been served with a copy of charges against him and an opportunity of being heard
    D. a list of those with complaints made against him *only*
    E. all of the above

21.___

22. A notary's oath of office is duly executed before
    A. the Secretary of State
    B. the county clerk
    C. the county clerk or his assistant
    D. an attorney
    E. any person authorized to administer an oath

22.___

23. The official character of a notary public is *certified* by
    A. the county clerk of the county in which the commission is filed
    B. any county clerk
    C. any county official
    D. another notary public
    E. at least two persons who have known the applicant for five years

23.___

24. When a notary files his autograph signature, the county clerk must
    A. be acquainted with his handwriting
    B. be authorized to accept the signature
    C. be acquainted with the notary either directly or through a third person
    D. believe the signature is genuine
    E. have proof that the signature is that of the notary's

24.___

25. A notary has authority to act in a county other than his county of residence
    A. if he files his oath with the county clerk of another county
    B. if he files his oath with the register of another county
    C. only with authorization of the Secretary of State
    D. at any time
    E. at no time

25.___

KEY (CORRECT ANSWERS)

1. A	6. E	11. D	16. A	21. C
2. B	7. E	12. D	17. A	22. E
3. D	8. A	13. D	18. C	23. A
4. D	9. E	14. E	19. E	24. D
5. A	10. E	15. A	20. C	25. D

TEST 2

DIRECTIONS: Each question or incomplete statement is followed by several suggested answers or completions. Select the one that BEST answers the question or completes the statement. *PRINT THE LETTER OF THE CORRECT ANSWER IN THE SPACE AT THE RIGHT.*

1. The fee for each notice of protest is 1.___
   A. $.25   B. $.75   C. $1.00   D. $2.00   E. $3.00

2. The fee for taking and certifying proof of execution of a written instrument is 2.___
   A. $.25   B. $2.00   C. $3.00   D. $5.00   E. $10.00

3. The fee for taking and certifying the acknowledgment or proof of execution of a written instrument when there is move than one person is 3.___
   A. $.25 for up to 5 person and $.10 for each additional person
   B. $.25 for one person and $.10 for each additional person
   C. $.50 for one person and $.25 for each additional person
   D. $.25 for one person and $.25 for each additional person
   E. $2.00 regardless of the number of persons

4. The physical presence of the affiant in the view of the notary is a requirement 4.___
   A. no longer adhered to today
   B. that is never waived
   C. that is sometimes waived
   D. that is waived only at the discretion of the notary
   E. for the performance of some notarial acts but not all

5. A notary is 5.___
   A. licensed   B. elected   C. certified
   D. commissioned   E. empowered

6. To ATTEST means to 6.___
   A. indicate genuineness by signing as a witness
   B. admit or recognize the existence of an agreement as binding and in full force
   C. describe acts performed in an official capacity
   D. make a statement
   E. give evidence under oath

7. It is NOT proper for a notary to 7.___
   A. advertise
   B. waive his fee
   C. raise his fee
   D. perform notarial acts for friends
   E. perform notarial acts for blood relatives

8. A paper on which writing or printing appears in a legal form, agreement or contract is called a(n) 8.___
   A. writ   B. deposition   C. letter of attorney
   D. notarial certificate   E. instrument

35

9. A NOTICE OF PROTEST is a notice given in connection with
   A. a formal order issued by a court of record
   B. demanding payment upon a negotiable instrument
   C. a false statement made under oath
   D. a negotiable instrument that has been dishonored
   E. a notary's failure to perform in accordance with his commission

10. A justice of the peace may take an oath ONLY if
    A. a notary is not available
    B. designated to do so by a notary
    C. the jurat is countersigned by a notary
    D. the oath is part of a marriage contract
    E. the oath is not required to be taken before a particular officer

11. Taking an acknowledgment differs from taking an affidavit in that
    A. it involves the administration of an oath
    B. it involves certification as to the identity and execution of the document
    C. the identity of the person appearing must be established
    D. the identity of the person need not be established
    E. there is NO difference

12. If a notary is convicted of a felony he will, as a notary, be
    A. removed from office
    B. fined
    C. suspended
    D. imprisoned
    E. unaffected

13. The privileges of a notary public may be delegated
    A. at no time to any person
    B. at all times to certain persons
    C. under certain circumstances
    D. sometimes
    E. when he sees fit and is satisfied to the other person's moral character

14. A notary may refuse to perform the duties of his office
    A. only if certain irregularities are present
    B. if the fee cannot be collected
    C. on certain days
    D. at certain hours
    E. at no time and under no circumstance

15. A notary is not authorized to protest any negotiable instrument owned by a corporation if he
    A. is a relative of any stockholder
    B. is a relative of any officer
    C. has a financial interest in the instrument
    D. is a stockholder or officer himself
    E. none of the above

16. A notary vacates his office when he
    A. resigns
    B. fails to qualify for reappointment
    C. moves from his area of jurisdiction
    D. all of the above
    E. none of the above

17. A notary can administer an oath to
    A. a person not personally known to him
    B. a person who does not personally appear before him
    C. a corporation
    D. a partnership
    E. none of the above

18. For any misconduct by a notary public in the performance of any of his powers, a notary shall be monetarily liable to
    A. the parties injured for all damages sustained by them
    B. only to the amount set by law
    C. the state only
    D. the courts only
    E. the notary is not liable

19. A notary may protest for nonpayment of
    A. bills of exchange   B. drafts
    C. checks   D. notes
    E. all of the above

20. The Secretary of State may designate _____ to sign commissions of notaries public.
    A. any notary public
    B. any person in the department of state
    C. any state official
    D. the county clerk of the county in which the notary resides
    E. any county clerk

21. Notarial acts are given force and solemnity by the
    A. moral character of the notary
    B. oath of office
    C. public respect for the office
    D. authorization and sanction of statute
    E. commission of office

22. Which of the following acts constitutes a felony? To
    A. practice any fraud
    B. certify falsely to the recording of deeds or other instruments
    C. deliver as true a certificate containing any statement he knows to be false
    D. practice deceit
    E. All of the above

23. Which of the following is NOT a true statement?   23.____
    A. It is the responsibility of the notary to ascertain the truth of the matters in relation to which he certifies
    B. The legal presumption that a notary has done his duty is unaffected when he does not recall the circumstances surrounding the oath
    C. A mere introduction at the time of the execution of the instrument is not sufficient evidence of identity
    D. The notary must have satisfactory evidence that the person making the acknowledgment is the person who executed it and is described therein
    E. Printed instruction directing use of a seal on papers for another state, does not mean that a seal may not be used on papers in this state

24. The purpose of the jurat is to give   24.____
    A. evidence that the oath was properly taken before a duly authorized officer
    B. the oath proper solemnity
    C. conclusive evidence of the oath's due administration
    D. legal presumption that the notary has done his duty
    E. all of the above

25. Which of the following statements is CORRECT?   25.____
    A. A notary can issue certified copies of public records
    B. A notary may certify to the authenticity of legal documents required to be files with foreign consular officers
    C. An attorney cannot act as a notary if he hasn't been commissioned as one
    D. A notary can only give advice on the law; he cannot practice it
    E. None of the above

KEY (CORRECT ANSWERS)

1. B	6. A	11. B	16. D	21. D
2. B	7. C	12. A	17. A	22. B
3. E	8. E	13. A	18. A	23. B
4. B	9. D	14. A	19. E	24. A
5. D	10. E	15. C	20. B	25. C

EXAMINATION SECTION
TEST 1

DIRECTIONS: Each question or incomplete statement is followed by several suggested answers or completions. Select the one that BEST answers the question or completes the statement. *PRINT THE LETTER OF THE CORRECT ANSWER IN THE SPACE AT THE RIGHT.*

1. In most states, other than New York, the license fees charged an applicant for the office of a notary public are determined by the
    A. county clerk
    B. applicant's previous experience
    C. population of the applicant's county of residence
    D. secretary of state

    1.____

2. A notary public
    A. can only be removed from office by impeachment
    B. must refuse to acknowledge the signature of someone whom the notary does not personally know
    C. may continue to act during a six-month period while waiting to renew an appointment
    D. must require that an affiant take an oral oath when acknowledging an affidavit

    2.____

3. When a notary public signs his or her signature to a document, he or she _____ the taking of the acknowledgement.
    A. certifies   B. swears
    C. records   D. affirms

    3.____

4. A notary public's rubber stamp seal should contain each of the following EXCEPT
    A. title
    B. commission expiration date
    C. coat of arms of the notary's state
    D. jurisdiction

    4.____

5. Authentication certificates are typically issued by a(n)
    A. notary public   B. attorney
    C. county clerk   D. county court justice

    5.____

6. Each of the following is a universal duty, power, or function of a notary public EXCEPT
    A. obtaining the acknowledgement of the party or parties that he, she, or they have signed the agreement or taken oath that they are aware of the contents of the agreement
    B. furnishing a certified copy of any public record notarized by him/her to anyone paying the proper fee
    C. making a written record of an act of notarization in an official record book kept for that purpose
    D. determining positively and beyond a shadow of a doubt that the party or parties to a written agreement are the party or parties they claim to be

    6.____

7. Someone who makes an oath to a written statement is a(n)
   A. notary public
   B. attestor
   C. affiant
   D. witness

8. Typically, a notary public must notify the secretary of state within _____ of any change of address of the notary's principal place of business.
   A. 10 days
   B. 30 days
   C. 90 days
   D. 6 months

9. When may a notary public demand a fee in advance?
   A. In any situation, under the judgment of the notary
   B. When the notary is not personally acquainted with one or more parties
   C. When the notary is in the presence of an attorney
   D. Never

10. *Sworn to before me this _____ day of _____, 20__* is a simple form of
    A. certificate of acknowledgement
    B. jurat
    C. authentication
    D. affidavit

11. All parties to an agreement, including the notary, should place their initials
    A. next to their respective signatures
    B. within the document letterhead
    C. in the lower right-hand corner of each page of the document
    D. in the margin of each page of the document

12. The BEST form of identification that can be presented to a notary is a(n)
    A. U.S. passport
    B. affidavit of birth
    C. birth certificate
    D. driver's license

13. If a notary can find no blank space on a document large enough to place the whole impression of a seal embosser, the notary should then attempt to place the seal
    A. in the margin
    B. on a separate, attached certificate
    C. near the document header
    D. directly over the signature(s) of the party (or parties)

14. A notary public who knowingly makes a false certificate is guilty of
    A. a felony
    B. misconduct
    C. a misdemeanor
    D. fraud

15. A notary public may NOT
    A. acknowledge an oath that is not sworn on the Bible
    B. be appointed for a two-year term
    C. administer an oath to a relative
    D. take the oath of a person in a language other than English

16. Which element typically appears at the end of a certificate of acknowledgement?
    A. Date of the acknowledgement
    B. Grantee signature
    C. Identification of the signer
    D. Testimonium clause

17. A notary should always print the letters _____ in the place over which a seal embosser is to be used.
    A. I.F.   B. L.S.   C. P.L.A.   D. T.C.

18. A notary is NOT empowered to
    A. draft a certificate of acknowledgement in states where the certificate isn't specified in codes
    B. certify the identity of the person who signed a document
    C. administer an oath of a state officer
    D. certify true copies of documents not in the notary's custody

19. A notary's duties are generally confined to those of a(n)
    A. advocate
    B. agent
    C. impartial witness
    D. broker

20. If a notary is to be removed for misconduct, this will typically be performed by the
    A. secretary of state
    B. sheriff
    C. governor
    D. county clerk

21. The witnessing of the execution of a written statement is known as
    A. certification
    B. conveyance
    C. affirmation
    D. attestation

22. A record of the date and time of an official act should be kept by a notary for the primary purpose of
    A. assisting in the conduct of any possible litigious action
    B. establishing the authenticity of an original document
    C. excluding any parties who were not present from notarization
    D. maintaining a reference in case one or more parties misplaces a copy of the agreement

23. A notarization states that a person or persons did each of the following EXCEPT
    A. issued an oral statement of intentions
    B. acknowledged to the notary that they signed an agreement or took an oath
    C. appeared before the notary
    D. took an oath and/or signed an agreement or statement

24. A person who has title to property is known as a(n)
    A. trustee
    B. grantee
    C. tenant
    D. freeholder

25. Which of the following is a term used to name a person who makes an affidavit?
    A. Advocate
    B. Plaintiff
    C. Witness
    D. Deponent

KEY (CORRECT ANSWERS)

1. C
2. A
3. A
4. C
5. C

6. B
7. D
8. B
9. D
10. B

11. C
12. A
13. A
14. A
15. D

16. D
17. B
18. A
19. C
20. A

21. A
22. B
23. A
24. D
25. D

TEST 2

DIRECTIONS: Each question or incomplete statement is followed by several suggested answers or completions. Select the one that BEST answers the question or completes the statement. *PRINT THE LETTER OF THE CORRECT ANSWER IN THE SPACE AT THE RIGHT.*

Questions 1-10.

DIRECTIONS: Questions 1 through 10 in Column I describe definitions listed in Column II. Write the letter of the CORRECT definition in the space at the right.

COLUMN I

1. A document whose purpose is to transfer money
2. One who grants rights, title, or interest in property to another
3. The performance of an act
4. The person to whom an oath or affirmation is administered
5. The offer of money, property, or services
6. To give as security without giving up title or posession
7. The act of demanding panent in connection with a negotiable instrument
8. A right, interest, or privilege to use the property of another
9. A formal act of adopting, approving, or sanctioning
10. To become due

COLUMN II

A. mature
B. hypothecate
C. feasance
D. accrue
E. plaintiff
F. executor
G. tender
H. affiant
I. ratification
J. trustor
K. presentment
L. easement
M. commercial paper
N. surety

1.___
2.___
3.___
4.___
5.___
6.___
7.___
8.___
9.___
10.___

11. A notary should NEVER issue a certified copy of a(n)
    A. contract of easement   B. deed
    C. birth certificate   D. conveyance

12. Which of the following typically notarizes the jurat in connection with a deposition?
    A. Court reporter   B. Attorney   C. Justice   D. Notary public

13. The purpose of a certificate of authority is to
    A. verify the identity of all parties involved in an agreement
    B. assist in notarizing a document in another state or country
    C. establish liability and/or subrogation rights in a particular contract
    D. notarize a contract of bottomry

14. A notary public may
    A. destroy a notary public record after 10 years
    B. use a facsimile signature stamp in signing acknowledgements or jurats
    C. prepare or draft declarations of homestead
    D. make a copy of a naturalization certificate, provided it is for a legitimate purpose

15. Which of the following is equivalent to an administration of an oath?
    A. Presentment of practice
    B. Certificate of authority
    C. A promissory note
    D. Acknowledgement of an instrument

16. If a document consists of more than one page, a notary should affix a portion of the official seal at or near the _____ of each page, in addition to the page on which the certificate appears or is stamped.
    A. margin   B. staple   C. bottom   D. top

17. The purpose of a notary bond is to
    A. protect the notary from any legal action resulting from his negligence
    B. protect any person who sustains damage as a result of the notary's improper performance of duty
    C. authenticate the identity of a notary
    D. insure the right of subrogation against any party involved in an agreement that proves to be fraudulent or false

18. The MOST important purpose of a seal embosser is to
    A. register the notary's jurisdiction
    B. record the parties involved in a notarized document
    C. verify that the document has been notarized
    D. prevent forgery

19. A jurat is affixed to a(n)
    A. affidavit
    B. lien
    C. certificate of acknowledgement
    D. transcript

20. Which of the following statements is TRUE? 20.___
    A. A notary may not make acknowledgement to an instrument if he has a financial interest in such instrument.
    B. A notary is authorized to advise any person coming to him as to the law pertaining to the papers presented for certification.
    C. If a notary shares his office with an attorney, she may share her fees with the attorney.
    D. If a notary is acquainted personally with the person making an affidavit, she may take the affidavit over the telephone.

21. A written order to pay a specified sum of money is a(n) 21.___
    A. warranty   B. bill of exchange
    C. presentment   D. dower

22. If a notary has been held liable for a negligent act, 22.___
    A. he or she may be removed
    B. the surety bond is automatically cancelled
    C. all notarizations made by the notary are void
    D. the notary is guilty of a misdemeanor

23. What is the term for a will that is written entirely in the hand of the person making the will? 23.___
    A. Holographic   B. Initiatory
    C. Seeded   D. Ministerial

24. A Recorder of Public Documents is PRIMARILY concerned with the issue of 24.___
    A. contracts
    B. births, deaths, and marriages
    C. certified copies
    D. identification verifications

25. Which of the following statements is FALSE? 25.___
    A. A notary can advise a friend to retain a particular attorney if the notary is not paid by the attorney for doing so.
    B. A notary who affixes a certificate to a false conveyance could be sued by a person who was defrauded by the conveyance.
    C. If a notary is somewhat familiar with a signature, he may take the acknowledgement on the word of a person who witnessed the signature.
    D. If a notary first states that she is not an attorney, she may then advise persons as to what the law is in a particular case.

KEY (CORRECT ANSWERS)

1. M
2. J
3. C
4. H
5. G

6. B
7. K
8. L
9. I
10. A

11. C
12. B
13. B
14. A
15. D

16. A
17. B
18. D
19. A
20. A

21. B
22. B
23. A
24. C
25. C

EXAMINATION SECTION
TEST 1

DIRECTIONS: Each question or incomplete statement is followed by several suggested answers or completions. Select the one that BEST answers the question or completes the statement. *PRINT THE LETTER OF THE CORRECT ANSWER IN THE SPACE AT THE RIGHT.*

1. A notary should NEVER, under any circumstances, notarize
    A. the signature of a business associate
    B. his/her own signature
    C. a unilateral contract
    D. the signature of a close relative

    1.___

2. A notary public who acts before taking and filing his or her oath of office is guilty of
    A. a felony
    B. perjury
    C. a misdemeanor
    D. fraud

    2.___

3. A certificate of _____ names a document that is fundamentally different in purpose from the others.
    A. acknowledgement
    B. official character
    C. authentication
    D. authority

    3.___

4. *Witness my hand and seal* is a short form of the
    A. jurat
    B. oath
    C. notarization
    D. testimonium clause

    4.___

5. Documents that can be used as evidence to prove title to real property are known as
    A. easements
    B. muniments
    C. commercial papers
    D. conveyances

    5.___

6. Typically, a notary is NOT permitted to make an acknowlegement to a(n)
    A. will
    B. conveyance
    C. declaration
    D. affidavit of birth

    6.___

7. A certificate of authority is issued by
    I. a pronotary
    II. the lieutenant governor
    III. the secretary of state
    IV. a state legislative body

    The CORRECT answer is:
    A. I, III   B. II, IV   C. I, II   D. III, IV

    7.___

8. If a legal form does not provide blank space to the left of the certificate for the notary's official seal, the notary should FIRST attempt to impress the seal
    A. near the document header
    B. in the margin
    C. in a blank space near the signature(s) of the party (or parties)
    D. over any bit of handwritten information

    8.___

9. If a notary is required to be bonded, the _____ is/are specified as principal(s).
   A. parties to any agreements notarized by the bonded notary
   B. bonding company
   C. county
   D. notary

10. The county in which an affidavit is sworn is known as a(n)
    A. venue
    B. juris
    C. arena
    D. quadrangle

11. Which of the following statements is TRUE?
    A. During such time as a notary public is available as a notary, she may not engage in other business during that same time.
    B. A notary may be imprisoned for misuse of notarial powers.
    C. The notary does not have to consider whether the affidavit is correct or false if the affiant is duly administered and takes an oath.
    D. An affirmation is less legally binding than an oath sworn on a Bible.

12. If a loose certificate has been stapled to a document, the required letters should be printed _____, and then squeeze the document and the certificate together with a seal embosser.
    A. only on the document header
    B. near the signatures on the document
    C. on the jurat
    D. between the staples on the margin

13. A notary is authorized to make corrections to a document.
    A. only under the direction of an attorney
    B. as long as all parties to the document are notified
    C. in any case, unless the document is a will
    D. under no circumstances

14. The certificate subjoined to any certificate or proof of acknowledgement is known as
    A. deposition
    B. authentication
    C. attestation
    D. certification

15. Which of the following terms is roughly synonymous with the term *witness*?
    A. Attest
    B. Affiant
    C. Endorse
    D. Litigant

16. Each of the following is an element of a typical certificate of acknowledgement EXCEPT
    A. jurisdiction of the notary
    B. identification of the signer
    C. notary bond number
    D. venue

17. The public official whose duties include keeping records of notaries is the 17.___
    I. secretary of state
    II. pronotary
    III. secretary of the interior
    IV. county clerk

    The CORRECT answer is:
    A. I, IV B. I, II C. II, III D. III, IV

18. A Proof of Acknowledgement is required when 18.___
    A. a witness refuses to take an oath
    B. a party appears without any form of identification
    C. the party who made the acknowledgement did not appear
    D. a party exercises signature by mark

19. What is the term for a court procedure in connection with the administration of 19.___
    affairs and distribution of property of a deceased person?
    A. Intestate B. Bequest
    C. Probate D. Attestation

20. A writing which transfers title to real property is termed a(n) 20.___
    A. conveyance B. assignment
    C. bequest D. endorsement

21. A rubber stamp should NEVER be used 21.___
    A. to add information to that provided by the seal embosser
    B. to disclose the notary's office or residence address
    C. for recording the notary's name
    D. for creating a facsimile of the notary's signature

22. A notary public 22.___
    A. must have the equivalent of a high school education
    B. is not entitled to a fee for administering the oath of office to a member of the state legislature
    C. working for a financial institution may agree to split his or her notarial fees with such financial institution
    D. may take a deposition on a legal holiday

23. The last person to examine a document before it is turned over to a recorder's office 23.___
    is the
    A. county clerk
    B. attorneys-in-fact for all parties involved
    C. notary public
    D. sheriff

24. An attestation is performed by a(n) 24.___
    A. affiant B. county clerk
    C. witness D. notary public

25. The purpose of an affirmation is to
    A. establish that the notary is personally acquainted with a party
    B. certify the authenticity of a written document
    C. uphold a notary's legal authority
    D. serve as the legal equivalent to an oath

KEY (CORRECT ANSWERS)

1.	B	11.	B
2.	C	12.	D
3.	A	13.	A
4.	D	14.	B
5.	B	15.	A
6.	A	16.	C
7.	A	17.	B
8.	C	18.	C
9.	D	19.	C
10.	A	20.	A

21. D
22. B
23. C
24. C
25. D

TEST 2

DIRECTIONS: Each question or incomplete statement is followed by several suggested answers or completions. Select the one that BEST answers the question or completes the statement. *PRINT THE LETTER OF THE CORRECT ANSWER IN THE SPACE AT THE RIGHT.*

1. A notarization must contain each of the following EXCEPT 1.___
   A. address of the notary
   B. secretary of state's facsimile signature
   C. jurisdiction
   D. commission expiration date

2. If a loose certificate is to be attached to a document, it should be stapled 2.___
   A. in the upper left-hand corner of the front page only
   B. over the blank space beneath the signatures
   C. in the upper right-hand corner of the last page only
   D. to the margins only

3. The notary's certification that a party appeared before him/her, took an oath, and signed an affidavit is the 3.___
   A. jurat   B. attestation
   C. seal   D. statement

4. If there is neither a blank space or a margin on a document that is large enough for the placement of a seal embosser's whole impression, the notary should then attempt to place a seal 4.___
   A. over information that is handwritten
   B. over information that is printed
   C. over information that is typewritten
   D. on a separate, attached document

5. If a notary is required to be bonded, the _____ is/are specified as surety or sureties. 5.___
   A. parties to any agreements notarized by the bonded notary
   B. bonding company
   C. county
   D. notary

Questions 6-15

DIRECTIONS: Questions 6 through 15 in Column I describe definitions for terms listed in Column II. Write the letter of the corresponding term for each definition in the space at the right.

COLUMN I

6. A document that transfers title of property
7. To void or cancel an agreement by declaring that it never existed
8. A formal request for rights or privileges
9. Ownership of property
10. A note payable when presented to the payor
11. Funds and/or documents entrusted to a third party with instructions
12. A formal document issued by the authority of a court
13. One who is responsible to manage or administer the funds and/or affairs of others
14. A declaration of abandonment of property rights
15. A written statement, signed by an official, describing acts performed in official capacity

COLUMN II

O. Sight draft
P. Petition
Q. Escrow
R. Certificate
S. Renunciation
T. Garnishment
U. Fee simple
V. Writ
W. Deed
X. Verification
Y. Fiduciary
Z. Rescind

16. Under any circumstances, a notary should avoid
    A. using a rubber stamp seal
    B. attempting to add aleatory contracts to the public record
    C. adding any description of how a document was notarized
    D. using a seal embosser on any page of a document other than the one bearing signatures

17. An affirmation may be given in place of an oath 17.____
    A. when a person has religious scruples against taking an oath
    B. when a person is not an American citizen
    C. when a person is illiterate
    D. under no circumstances

18. The person for whom notarial acts are performed by a notary is BEST described as 18.____
    the notary's
    A. customer   B. constituent
    C. agent   D. client

19. A notary is authorized to 19.____
    A. draw a will
    B. help prepare business bankruptcy papers
    C. administer an oath to himself/herself
    D. offer legal advice to a party in an agreement

20. A notary's MOST important obligation to the public can be described as 20.____
    A. exposing and reporting the malfeasance of parties within the community
    B. providing sworn documents for the public record
    C. judging what acts constitute the practice of law and what acts constitute the practice of a notary public
    D. resolving partisan disputes within the community

21. Which of the following statements is TRUE? 21.____
    A. When a person is appointed notary public from his or her home county, it is mandatory that she file an additional certificate in any other county in which she may wish to practice.
    B. Authentication consists of words placed directly after the signature in an affidavit.
    C. In certain circumstances, notaries may certify the authenticity of legal documents.
    D. A woman notary may continue to use her maiden name indefinitely after she marries.

22. A notary bond is typically signed by the 22.____
    A. county clerk and the notary
    B. notary and any parties to a notarized agreement
    C. notary and the attorney-in-fact for the bonding company
    D. secretary of state and residing pronotary

23. Which of the following is a notary public usually NOT authorized to do? 23.____
    A. Notarize the signature of a relative
    B. Solemnize a marriage
    C. Perform an acknowledgement on a Saturday
    D. Notarize a contract of adhesion

24. If corrections are made to a document, the notary and all parties should add their 24.____
    initials
    A. to a new, corrected document
    B. in the margin next to each correction
    C. to the accompanying jurat
    D. in the lower right-hand corner of all pages containing corrections

25. Which of the following statements is TRUE? 25.___
   A. Any attorney may act as a notary.
   B. A notary may advertise in papers that (s)he is an appointed notary public.
   C. If an affiant states that the signature on a particular document is hers, she does not have to sign in the presence of a notary.
   D. A notary's license fees depend on the volume of fees collected during the notary's previous appointment.

KEY (CORRECT ANSWERS)

1.	B	11.	Q
2.	D	12.	V
3.	A	13.	Y
4.	B	14.	S
5.	B	15.	R
6.	W	16.	C
7.	Z	17.	A
8.	P	18.	B
9.	U	19.	B
10.	O	20.	C

21. D
22. C
23. B
24. B
25. B

EXAMINATION SECTION
TEST 1

DIRECTIONS: Each question or incomplete statement is followed by several suggested answers or completions. Select the one that BEST answers the question or completes the statement. *PRINT THE LETTER OF THE CORRECT ANSWER IN THE SPACE AT THE RIGHT.*

1. A faxed or photocopied document may
   A. be notarized if the notary recognizes the signer
   B. be notarized if it is signed after it is faxed or photocopied
   C. be notarized if the notary is personally acquainted with the signe
   D. never be notarized

1.___

2. Which of the following is a document that makes known a person's wishes about life-sustaining medical treatment?
   A. Last Will and Testament
   B. Power of Attorney
   C. Living Will
   D. Contingency Contract

2.___

3. A jurat
   I. compels the document signer to be truthful
   II. requires the administration of an oath of affirmation
   III. could initiate a process resulting in a criminal conviction for perjury if the signer is found to be lying

   A. I only
   B. I and II
   C. I, II and III
   D. None of the above

3.___

4. Which of the following is a term used to denote a special seal, most often used internationally, that is attached to a notarized and county-certified document and certifies its status as a true copy of the original?
   A. Hague
   B. Apostille
   C. Jurat
   D. Codicil

4.___

5. A loan repayment schedule that is designed on a decreasing basis, with a set amount toward interest and balance toward the principal until each are paid in full, is a(n)
   A. graduated repayment
   B. barratry
   C. consolidation
   D. amortization

5.___

6. Under New York law, a notary public who is not a licensed attorney may NOT
   I. advertise or represent to anyone that she has powers or rights not given to the notary by the laws under which she was appointed
   II. divide his fees with a lawyer or accept any part of a lawyer's fee
   III. ask for or receive any legal business to refer to a lawyer with whom she has any business connection or receives any consideration for sending the lawyer business
   IV. give advice on the law

   A. I nor II
   B. II, III nor IV
   C. III nor IV
   D. I, II, III nor IV

Questions 7 and 8 refer to the following situation: A bank has not received rental payments for a safe deposit box for several months, despite several attempts to reach the lessee, Mr. Johnson. The bank then terminates the lease on the box.

7. The bank is authorized, in the presence of a notary public, to open Mr. Johnson's safe deposit box and inventory its contents, after at least _____ have passed since giving notice to the Mr. Johnson that the box would be opened.

   A. 10 days
   B. 30 days
   C. 90 days
   D. 6 months

8. After the contents of the safe deposit box have been inventoried, the notary public must file with the bank, under seal, a certificate that states the date of the opening of the box, Mr. Johnson's full name, and a list of the contents.
   Within _____ of the opening of the safe deposit box, the notary public must mail a copy of this certificate to Mr. Johnson's last known postal address.

   A. 48 hours
   B. 10 days
   C. 30 days
   D. 90 days

9. A notary public could be described as a(n)
   I. witness of notarial writings and signatures
   II. advocate for the state
   III. a public officer

   A. I and II
   B. I and III
   C. II and III
   D. I, II and III

10. The usual term for an individual known personally by the notary public and signer who affirms or swears to the identity of the signer is the _____ witness.

    A. hearsay
    B. credible
    C. eye
    D. subscribing

11. A notary serves

    A. only customers who reside in the notary's county of commission
    B. mostly friends and family
    C. only customers who are directed to the notary by supervising authorities
    D. all members of the public

12. The amount that remains to be paid on a loan, minus interest, is the

    A. equity
    B. precedent
    C. principal
    D. service fee

13. A properly maintained notarial journal should include

    I. the document signer's signature
    II. the date and time of notarization
    III. a description of the procedure used to verify the signature
    IV. the document signer's address

    A. I and II
    B. I, II and IV
    C. II, III and IV
    D. I, II, III and IV

14. New York notaries are empowered to

    I. receive and certify powers of attorney
    II. certify copies of official documents
    III. protest bills of exchange for non-payment
    IV. notarize last wills and testaments

    E. I only
    F. I and III
    G. III and IV
    H. I, II, III and IV

15. A notary public certifies a Proof of Execution by a Subscribing Witness. The statutory fee in New York for this service is

    A. $.75
    B. $1
    C. $2
    D. $10

16. On a Sunday, a notary public may NOT
    A. administer an oath
    B. take an affidavit
    C. take a deposition in a civil proceeding
    D. any of the above

17. Which of the following is LEAST likely to be acceptable as a signing in representative capacity?
    A. A partner on behalf of a partnership
    B. A parent on behalf of a child
    C. A CEO for a corporation
    D. An attorney-in-fact on behalf of a principal

18. The following appears in a certificate of acknowledgement.

    Subscribed and sworn to before me, the undersigned Notary Public within and for the State of New York and County of x, this_____day of_____, _____.

    The x in the portion above should be the county
    A. where the signer resides
    B. where the document originated
    C. in which the notary is standing
    D. in which the notary is commissioned

19. A(n)_____is a historical summary of all the recorded instruments and proceedings that affect the title of a property.
    A. deed
    B. abstract
    C. survey
    D. escrow

20. A notary public who buys an Errors and Omissions policy is protected against
    A. civil actions by signers who are defrauded as a result of a notarized transaction
    B. any and all errors or omissions committed while notarizing
    C. any and all administrative errors committed by the office of the county clerk
    D. error or omissions committed unintentionally while notarizing

21. Under New York law, a notary public may
    A. only advertise in print for notary services
    B. advertise only if he or she is a practicing attorney who can provide legal advice
    C. advertise in any medium, for any and all services the notary is authorized to perform under state notary law
    D. never advertise his or her services

22. John, a notary public, is also a stockholder in XYZ Corporation Which of the following may John legally and ethically perform, under limited circumstance?
    I. Take the acknowledgement of any party to a written instrument executed by XYZ Corporation
    II. Administer an oath to an officer of XYZ Corporation
    III. Protest for non-acceptance a check held by XYZ Corporation

A. I only
B. I or II
C. I, II or III
D. None of the above

23. _____ is the act of producing a negotiable or security instrument for payment or acceptance.

   A. Deposit
   B. Presentment
   C. Tender
   D. Conveyance

24. Anything of value given to induce entrance into a contract is denoted broadly by the term

   A. money
   B. novation
   C. consideration
   D. conveyance

25. New York law provides that when an applicant for the office of notary public is not a practicing attorney or a court clerk, the Secretary of State shall satisfy himself or herself that the applicant is of good moral character, is adequately educated, and is familiar with the duties of the notary public.

   Herbert Hugo, who earned a GED and is a member of the Army Reserve, underwent this requirement when he was appointed to the office of notary public. When Mr. Hugo was deployed overseas, his commission as a notary ended. He returned to New York and was honorably discharged from service after two consecutive deployments.
   Which of the following is TRUE?

   A. If he applies for reappointment as a notary within 6 months of his discharge, the qualifying requirements may be waived.
   B. If he applies for reappointment as a notary within 1 year of his discharge, the qualifying requirements may be waived.
   C. He must undergo the application process as if he had never before applied for or held the office of notary public.
   D. As a veteran who served during wartime, he is automatically eligible for the office of notary public, and need never again prove that he has satisfied the qualifying requirements.

KEY (CORRECT ANSWERS)

1. B	6. D	11. D	16. C	21. C
2. C	7. B	12. C	17. B	22. C
3. C	8. B	13. D	18. D	23. B
4. B	9. B	14. B	19. B	24. C
5. D	10. B	15. B	20. D	25. B

TEST 2

DIRECTIONS: Each question or incomplete statement is followed by several suggested answers or completions. Select the one that BEST answers the question or completes the statement. *PRINT THE LETTER OF THE CORRECT ANSWER IN THE SPACE AT THE RIGHT.*

1. A New York notary public who moves out of state and closes down his or her place of business in New York must _____ his or her notary commission.

    A. transfer
    B. renew
    C. maintain
    D. resign

2. A written statement, signed and sworn to by the person appearing before the notary, is a(n)

    A. acknowledgement
    B. jurat
    C. affidavit
    D. certificate

3. In most cases, the best credible identifying witness is a

    A. disinterested party who knows both the signer and the notary
    B. relative who knows both the signer and the notary
    C. person named in the document
    D. stranger who knows neither the signer nor the notary

4. A notary's own oath and surety bond are filed with the

    A. District Attorney
    B. Circuit Clerk
    C. County Assessor
    D. County Clerk

5. The transfer of a mortgage from one person to another is known as

    A. assumption
    B. conveyance
    C. assignment
    D. remittance

6. The act of notarization

    I. certifies that a signature is made willingly and freely
    II. certifies that a document or statement is true or accurate
    III. proves the signer either appeared before the notary public or is a person who has otherwise spoken directly and verifiably to the notary public
    IV. validates or legalizes a document

A. I only
B. I and II
C. I, III and IV
D. None of the above

7. What is the term for a map that shows the exact legal boundaries of a property and includes improvements, easements, encroachments, and other features?

    A. Grid
    B. Site map
    C. Plat
    D. Survey

8. A notary who is found negligent in his or her notarial duties may face _____ penalties.

    I. administrative
    II. civil
    III. criminal

    A. I only
    B. I or II
    C. II or III
    D. I, II or III

9. Under New York Law, a notary who notarizes after his or her commission is guilty of a(n)

    A. Class A misdemeanor
    B. unclassified misdemeanor
    C. Class C felony
    D. tort

10. In New York, a(n) _____ is a means by which a grantor disclaims any interest the grantor might have in a piece of real property, and passes that claim to another person without professing that the grantor's claim was actually valid.

    A. release
    B. warranty
    C. grant
    D. quitclaim

11. NEITHER a Commissioner of Deeds NOR a Notary Public in New York may

    A. take a deposition in a civil court case
    B. notarize a loan signature
    C. notarize a relative's signature
    D. notarize a marriage contract

12. Which of the following statements is TRUE?

    A. There are no known circumstances under which a notary can legally notarize his or her own signature.
    B. If a son acts as a subscribing witness for a parent on a document in which he is named, there is no conflict of interest.
    C. It is a conflict of interest for a notary to notarize a petition for a political candidate for whom the notary plans to vote.
    D. There are some circumstances under which it may be a good idea to notarize for one's spouse.

13. A person who intentionally makes false statements under oath is liable to prosecution for

    A. fraud
    B. conspiracy
    C. perjun
    D. extortion

14. In the _____ clause at the end of a will, witnesses clarify that the instrument has been executed before them.

    A. residuary
    B. indemnification
    C. attestation
    D. supremacy

15. A self-inking stamp may be used by a notary public on notarized documents to record the

    I. expiration date of the commission
    II. an impression of the notary's signature
    III. commission number
    IV. notary's name as commissioned

    A. I or III
    B. I, III or IV
    C. III only
    D. I, II, III or IV

16. A New York notary public is authorized to

    I. take a deposition in a civil proceeding
    II. take the public acknowledgement of parties and witnesses to a written contract of marriage
    III. administer the oath of a public officer
    IV. certify that a signer is who he/she claims to be

    A. I and II
    B. I, III and IV
    C. II and IV
    D. I, II, III and IV

17. A hearing or examination in the presence of, or on papers filed by, one party and in the absence of another is described as

    A. *a fortiori*
    B. *ad hominem*
    C. *persona non grata*
    D. *ex parte*

18. Ned Stone, a notary public, lives in rural Niagara County but works at a bank in downtown Buffalo, in Erie County. At the bank in Buffalo, notarized documents often need to have Ned's signature authenticated. To have this done in Buffalo, Ned should

    A. move to Erie County
    B. have the Niagara County Clerk send an authentication by fax
    C. file a Certificate of Official Character with Erie County
    D. complete a new application for a commission in Erie County

19. An applicant for the office of notary public in New York must have completed, at the minimum, a _____ education or the equivalent

    A. 6th grade
    B. high school
    C. two-year (community) college
    D. four-year college

20. An index of notarial commissions and official signatures is maintained by the

    A. Office of the Governor
    B. secretary of state
    C. county clerk
    D. county commissioner

21. Legally, a deposition is considered to be false when

    I. no oath or affirmation has been administered or taken
    II. the affiant has not affirmed to it
    III. the deponent has not sworn to it
    IV. the deponent committed perjury

    A. I, III or IV
    B. I or III
    C. IV only
    D. I, II, III or IV

22. In New York, the main difference between a notary public and a commissioner of deeds is one of

    A. the range of empowerments
    B. length of commission
    C. geographic jurisdiction
    D. difficulty in obtaining a commission

23. A(n) _____ is a sum of money given to ensure payment or an advance of funds in the processing of a loan.

    A. deposit
    B. bond
    C. surety
    D. bailment

24. New York law provides that when an applicant for the office of notary public is not a practicing attorney or a court clerk, the Secretary of State shall satisfy himself or herself that the applicant is of good moral character, is adequately educated, and is familiar with the duties of the notary public. This requirement is waived for subsequent reappointment if a notary public applies before the end of his or her commission, or within _____ of the termination of his or her commission.

    A. 30 days
    B. 90 days
    C. 6 months
    D. 1 year

25. When a notarized document will be sent to another state to be used in a court of law, the New York Secretary of State typically issues a certificate attached the document. This attached certification is a(n)

    A. apostille
    B. enjoinment
    C. authentication
    D. certificate of official character

KEY (CORRECT ANSWERS)

1. D	6. A	11. D	16. E	21. D
2. C	7. D	12. A	17. D	22. C
3. A	8. D	13. C	18. C	23. A
4. D	9. A	14. C	19. A	24. C
5. C	10. D	15. B	20. C	25. C

TEST 3

DIRECTIONS: Each question or incomplete statement is followed by several suggested answers or completions. Select the one that BEST answers the question or completes the statement. *PRINT THE LETTER OF THE CORRECT ANSWER IN THE SPACE AT THE RIGHT.*

1. An elderly family friend has designated a notary public as her representative in a power of attorney document. The notary may
   A. not notarize the document, because he is named in it
   B. not notarize the document, because he is personally acquainted with the signer
   C. notarize it, because he is the document signer
   D. notarize it only if the friend requests it

   1.___

2. Geographically, a notary's jurisdiction is
   A. citywide
   B. county wide
   C. statewide
   D. nationwide

   2.___

3. A signed mortgage or deed of trust is also known as a
   A. collateral
   B. security instrument
   C. certificate of authenticity
   D. promissory note

   3.___

4. In notarial terms, "execute" means to
   A. authenticate a person's identity
   B. make or complete a signature
   C. give legal instructions
   D. provide oral testimony under oath but not in court

   4.___

5. In New York, a notary public's term of commission is_____years.
   A. 4
   B. 5
   C. 10
   D. 15

   5.___

6. To "_____title" is to declare that a certain person is the legal owner of the real property in dispute.
   A. rebut
   B. quiet
   C. cloud
   D. quash

   6.___

65

7. The county clerk's signature and seal upon a certificate of official character of a notary public, or of a county clerk upon a certificate of authentication of the signature and acts of a notary public, may be
   I. a printed facsimile
   II. stamped
   III. engraved
   IV. photographed

   A. I only
   B. I or II
   C. I, II, or III
   D. I, II, III or IV

8. In order to qualify for an appointment to the office of notary public, an applicant must take an oath of office in the presence of

   A. a New York notary public
   B. the secretary of state
   C. the county clerk or sheriff
   D. a commissioned peace officer

9. An instrument that is made subsequent to a will, and which modifies the will to an extent, is a(n)

   A. living will
   B. codicil
   C. ademption
   D. holographic will

10. To_____is to grant the rights of usage of real property for a given term, for life, or at will.

    A. mortgage
    B. lease
    C. deed
    D. convey

11. Upon a notary's appointment, a dated copy of the commission, a certified copy or the original of the oath of office and the official signature, and a portion of the application fee shall be transmitted to the county clerk

    A. within 10 days of the granting of the commission
    B. within 30 days of the granting of the commission
    C. by the 1st day of the following month.
    D. by the 10th day of the following month

12. The maintenance of a notarial journal
    I. should involve the completion of an entry after every notarial act
    II. documents that the notary took reasonable steps to verify the signer's identity
    III. is required by New York law

A. I and II
B. II only
C. II and III
D. I, II and III

13. A defendant in a lawsuit asserts that the plaintiff has failed to exert legal rights within a timely manner, thereby releasing the defendant from an original claim. The defendant is invoking the legal principle of

    A. laches
    B. statute of limitations
    C. *habeus corpus*
    D. *respondeat superior*

14. What is the term for a condition that must be met before a contract is legally binding?

    A. Contingency
    B. Exemption
    C. Obligation
    D. Consideration

15. A person who "attests" is

    A. recognizing a document by a subscribing witness
    B. taking an oath or affirmation
    C. certifying a copy of an original public record
    D. witnessing the signing of a written document

16. The _____ rate is the stated interest rate on a promissory note.

    A. target
    B. note
    C. true
    D. prime

17. Typically, a certified copy of a recorded document is obtained from

    A. the public office that originally issued the document
    B. a notary public
    C. the county clerk
    D. a commissioner of deeds

18. A signer presents a notary public with a deed for real property in New York. The venue for this deed is the county and state where

    A. the notary was commissioned
    B. the signer lives
    C. the notary is taking the acknowledgement
    D. the real property is located

19. Hannah Gluck, a New York notary, is also a member of the New York bar. In notarizing a signature, she may substitute the words "notary public" with

    I. Attorney at Law/Notary Public
    II. Counselor at Law
    III. Attorney at Law
    IV. Attorney and Counselor at Law

    A. I only
    B. I, II or III
    C. IV only
    D. I, II, III or IV

20. What is the term for a person who promises to be responsible for the debt of another person if that person fails to pay the debt on time?

    A. guarantor
    B. obligor
    C. guardian *ad litem*
    D. executor

21. A man who makes a will is known as a

    A. probate
    B. codicil
    C. testator
    D. intestate

22. Every affidavit or acknowledge certificate must include the _____ for all notarial acts.

    A. venue
    B. city or township
    C. fee charged
    D. time of notarization

23. For which of the following services would a notary public NOT be entitled to a fee?

    A. Administering an ordinary oath in connection with an affidavit
    B. Certifying the proof of execution of a written instrument
    C. Administering an oath of office to a member of the legislature
    D. Protesting for the non-payment of a note

24. In April of 2007, a signer was charged $10 by a notary for the taking of a single acknowledgement. Under New York law, the signer is entitled to damages equaling

    A. $8
    B. $24
    C. $100
    D. $500

25. Serena Smith is an attorney who practices regularly in New York State and holds the office of notary public. She recently moved to Pittsfield, Massachusetts, but still maintains her legal practice out of her office in Albany.

   Which of the following statements is/are true?
   - I. Serena Smith can no longer hold the office of notary public in New York.
   - II. She must re-apply for the office of notary public.
   - III. She can remain a New York notary but must inform the Secretary of State of her change of residence.
   - IV. In New York, she is considered to be a resident of Albany County.

   A. I only
   B. I and II
   C. II, III and IV
   D. III and IV

KEY (CORRECT ANSWERS)

1. A	6. B	11. D	16. B	21. C
2. C	7. D	12. A	17. A	22. A
3. B	8. A	13. A	18. C	23. C
4. B	9. B	14. A	19. C	24. B
5. A	10. B	15. D	20. A	25. D

EXAMINATION SECTION
TEST 1

DIRECTIONS: Each question or incomplete statement is followed by several suggested answers or completions. Select the one that BEST answers the question or completes the statement. *PRINT THE LETTER OF THE CORRECT ANSWER IN THE SPACE AT THE RIGHT.*

1. A beneficial interest in a transaction 1.___
   A. only applies if the notary stands to make a financial gain from the transaction
   B. does not apply if the notary is an officer of a corporation involved in the transaction
   C. makes it illegal for the notary to notarize signatures on any documents associated with the transaction
   D. is affected by travel fees

2. A notary public has been asked to notarize a blind person's signature. The person has been positively identified. The notary must 2.___
   A. place in the notary journal a waiver, signed by the blind person, stating that he is signing a document that he cannot reasonably be expected to have read
   B. place in the notary journal a statement, signed by the blind person, that he fully understands the contents of the document he is signing
   C. decline to notarize the signature, given that the person cannot read
   D. read the entire document to the person before notarizing his signature

3. The following appears in a certificate of acknowledgement. 3.___

   State of New York
   County of_____

   In the blank above, the notary should identify the venue as the county

   A. where the signer resides
   B. where the document originated
   C. in which the notary is standing
   D. in which the notary is commissioned

4. Of the following, which would be eligible to hold the office of notary public in New York State? 4.___
   I. Someone who violated the federal selective service and training act of 1940.
   II. A commissioner of elections
   III. Someone who has been removed from office as a commissioner of deeds
   IV. A county sheriff

   A. I, II and IV
   B. II only
   C. II and IV
   D. V only

71

5. A notary's surety bond is filed to protect the
   A. notary
   B. parties who receive the notary's services
   C. county of commission
   D. state

6. A_____is a written agreement that guarantees a real estate buyer a specific interest rate on repayment of a loan that is closed within a specified period of time.
   A. lock-in
   B. bind-over
   C. block
   D. warranty deed

7. A notary is appointed on August 11, 2007. His commission expires on
   A. August 11, 2008
   B. September 1, 2011
   C. August 11, 2011
   D. August 1, 2012

8. A person appointed by the court to manage the estate of a deceased person who left no will is a(n)
   A. administrator
   B. executor
   C. probate
   D. testator

9. In order for a conveyance to be acceptable to a county recording officer, the conveyance must be
   A. stamped with a notary seal
   B. written in English
   C. witnessed
   D. filed with the assessor

10. The type of deed conveyed by most mortgage contracts is the_____ _____deed.
    A. release
    B. quitclaim
    C. bailment
    D. warranty

11. A person who assumes the responsibility for the care of a minor's care and/or property is a
    A. guardian
    B. foster parent
    C. ward
    D. steward

12. A properly maintained notarial journal
    I.   cannot be used in the investigation or prosecution of allegations of fraud
    II. protects the notary from unfounded allegations of wrongdoing by documenting that reasonable care was exercised in performing every step of the notarization
    III. facilitates quicker resolutions of disputes outside of court
    IV. protects document signers and other parties to transactions from risk if the document is lost, wrongfully altered or challenged

    A. I and II
    B. II and IV
    C. II, III and IV
    D. I, II, III and IV

13. The general authority of a notary public is outlined in the _____ Law section of New York State's Notary Public License Law.
    A. Civil Practice
    B. Executive
    C. Public Officers
    D. Real Property

14. A(n) _____ is a preliminary agreement that is secured by a deposit, and under which a buyer offers to purchase real estate.
    A. good faith offer
    B. earnest
    C. verbal agreement
    D. binder

15. A(n) _____ is anything that affects or limits the fee simple title to a property, such as a mortgage, easement, lease, or restriction.
    A. encumbrance
    B. escrow
    C. enjoinment
    D. estoppel

16. _____ is the process of evaluating a loan application to calculate the risk involved for the lender.
    A. Underwriting
    B. Appraisal
    C. Concession
    D. Assessment

17. Greg, who works at North American Title, needs to get his supervisor's signature notarized on a loan document. The supervisor is unable to appear in person to the notary. Greg is a personal acquaintance of Nancy, a notary. He should request a(n) _____ notarization from Nancy.
    A. Credible Witness Acknowledgement
    B. Oath
    C. Proof of Execution
    D. Jurat

18. The Latin abbreviation_____is printed near the venue of a certificate of acknowledgement, in order to specify the particular place within a city and/or county where the notarial act was performed.

    A. S.S.
    B. A.L.
    C. L.S.
    D. T.W.

19. A notary uses a seal to notarize a document. Under New York law, the document requires_____to be considered officially notarized.

    I.   the name of the notary
    II. the words "Notary Public for the State of New York"
    III. the commission expiration date
    IV. nothing further

    A. I and II
    B. II only
    C. I, II and III
    D. IV only

20. What is the term for a written instrument given to pass title of personal property from seller to purchaser?

    A. Contract of bailment
    B. Bill of lading
    C. Mortgage
    D. Bill of sale

21. Which of the following is NOT acceptable as a form of identification for the purpose of verifying a document signer?

    A. Social Security card
    B. Green card or resident alien card
    C. valid passport
    D. out-of-state driver's license with photo

22. A notary public is commissioned in the county in which he or she

    A. resides
    B. conducts most of his or her business
    C. submits the application
    D. chooses to be commissioned

23. A person who commits forgery on a notarized document is guilty of a

    A. Class B misdemeanor
    B. Class C misdemeanor
    C. Class D felony
    D. Class E felony

24. A(n) _____ clause permits the placing of a mortgage at a later date that takes priority over an existing mortgage.
    A. subjunctive
    B. assumption
    C. acceleration
    D. subordination

25. A notary public who is an attorney at law regularly admitted to practice in the State of New York may
    I. administer an oath or affirmation to her client
    II. take that affidavit or acknowledgement of her client
    III. not hold the office of notary public in any other state
    IV. charge fees in excess of the customary fees charged by a notary public for certain services

    A. I only
    B. I or II
    C. I, II or III
    D. I, II, III or IV

KEY (CORRECT ANSWERS)

1. C	6. A	11. A	16. A	21. A
2. D	7. C	12. C	17. C	22. A
3. C	8. A	13. B	18. A	23. C
4. B	9. B	14. D	19. A	24. D
5. D	10. D	15. A	20. D	25. B

TEST 2

DIRECTIONS: Each question or incomplete statement is followed by several suggested answers or completions. Select the one that BEST answers the question or completes the statement. *PRINT THE LETTER OF THE CORRECT ANSWER IN THE SPACE AT THE RIGHT.*

1. If any doubts are raised about a notary's impartiality during a notarization, the notary should
   A. proceed or decline according to his or her own assessment of impartiality
   B. proceed if the signer declares it to be acceptable
   C. decline to accept a fee
   D. decline to notarize

   1.___

2. Evidence of a mortgage loan is placed on public record at the
   A. local library
   B. lender's office
   C. county clerk's office
   D. county assessor's office

   2.___

3. The transcript of an oral witness's testimony, taken out of court but under oath, is a(n)
   A. attestation
   B. affidavit
   C. authentication
   D. deposition

   3.___

4. In New York, notaries public are commissioned by the
   A. governor
   B. secretary of state
   C. county clerk
   D. county sheriff

   4.___

5. Which of the following is NOT an example of personal property?
   A. Automobile
   B. Negotiable instruments
   C. Household goods
   D. Land

   5.___

6. Franklin, a New York notary, lives in Utica, in Oneida County. His uncle John, who lives Canandaigua, in Ontario County, calls Franklin and asks him to notarize a document that will allow John to receive treatment at the VA hospital in Canandaigua. Franklin may legally
   I. hire a notary in Oneida County over the telephone to visit his uncle and notarize his signature
   II. refuse to notarize the document on the grounds that John is a blood relative
   III. travel to Oneida County and notarize his uncle's signature there
   IV. have John mail him the signed document for notarization

   6.___

A. I or II
B. II or III
C. III only
D. I, II, III or IV

7. The usual term for the witness who appears to a notary to prove, by taking an oath or affirmation, that an absent signer signed a document or executed an instrument, is a(n)_____witness.

    A. affirming
    B. credible
    C. favorable
    D. subscribing

8. In New York, taking acknowledgements over the telephone is

    A. permissible if the notary is personally acquainted with the person giving the acknowledgement
    B. permissible only if the notary has the original document in hand, signed in the person's own hand
    C. a misdemeanor
    D. a felony

9. An improperly recorded deed is described as a(n)_____deed.

    A. wild
    B. clouded
    C. unbound
    D. blocked

10. The use of seals by notaries public in New York

    A. is strongly discouraged by the Department of State
    B. is not required by law
    C. is by itself sufficient for notarization
    D. is limited to notaries public who are also practicing attorneys

11. Stella Martin, a New York notary public, recently moved out of state. Which of the following is TRUE?

    A. She can maintain her commission in New York if she continues to maintain a place of business in New York.
    B. She can maintain her commission in New York if she keeps a P.O. box in New York.
    C. She cannot maintain her commission in New York if she accepts a commission as a notary public in another state.
    D. She must resign her commission as notary public.

12. Under New York Notary Licensing Law, the validity of a certificate or other notarized act is protected in spite of certain defects. Defects whose consequences are protected by the errors and omissions clause include

I. fraud
II. the taking of an action outside the jurisdiction where the notary public was authorized to act
III. the expiration of the notary's commission
IV. the misspelling of the notary's name on his or her commission

A. I only
B. I and II
C. II, III and IV
D. I, II, III and IV

13. A notary takes an oath from 2 people and takes a single Proof of Execution. For these services, he may charge a fee of

A. $2
B. $4
C. $6
D. $8

14. What is the term for a formal notice that asks a court to suspend action until the party that filed a challenge can be heard?

A. Caveat
B. Estoppel
C. Sanction
D. Injunction

15. In New York, a notary public who is not a licensed attorney and gives legal advice may be punished for criminal contempt by the_____Court.

A. Supreme
B. Superior
C. District
D. Lower

16. New York notaries are empowered to

I. administer oaths and affirmations
II. take affidavits and depositions
III. demand acceptance of foreign bills of exchange
IV. receive and certify acknowledgements

A. I only
B. I and II
C. I, II and IV
D. I, II, III and IV

17. Which of the following types of documents can be used as evidence to prove ownership of real property?

A. Conveyance
B. Warranty
C. Easement
D. Commercial paper

18. What is the legal term for the improper performance of an act that a person is legally authorized to perform?

    A. Misfeasance
    B. Sabotage
    C. Malfeasance
    D. Nonfeasance

19. A jurat notarial wording certificate indicates that the

    A. signer willingly signed the document
    B. notary is personally acquainted with the signer
    C. signer gave an oath or affirmation
    D. notary has not beneficial interest in the transaction

20. What is the term for a person who conveys an interest in real property?

    A. Obligor
    B. Obligee
    C. Grantor
    D. Grantee

21. A(n)_____is performed when a subscribing witness appears before a notary public with a document to be notarized.

    A. Proof of Execution
    B. Authentication
    C. Certificate of Acknowledgement
    D. Certificate of Official Character

22. The notary's entitlement to a fee is the same amount for each of the following, EXCEPT for

    A. certifying an oath or affirmation
    B. notarizing a notice of non-acceptance or non-payment
    C. administering an oath or affirmation
    D. taking and certifying the acknowledgement or proof of execution of a written instrument

23. The_____typically issues authentication certificates that identify the authority of a notary public.

    A. secretary of state
    B. notary public
    C. district attorney
    D. county clerk

24. A non-resident of New York

    A. cannot be commissioned as a New York notary
    B. can notarized New York documents from out-of-state if he or she has a valid notarial commission
    C. can accept the office of notary public, but must designate the Secretary of State as the person on whom process can be served in his or her behalf
    D. can accept the office of notary public, but cannot notarize documents on behalf of any residents of New York State

25. In New York, a notary public is NEVER permitted to notarize   25.____
    I.   for close friends
    II. on a legal holiday
    III. his or her own signature
    IV. for family members

    A. I or II
    B. II or IV
    C. III only
    D. I, II, III or IV

KEY (CORRECT ANSWERS)

1. D	6. C	11. A	16. D	21. A
2. C	7. D	12. C	17. A	22. B
3. D	8. C	13. C	18. A	23. D
4. B	9. A	14. A	19. C	24. C
5. D	10. B	15. A	20. C	25. C

TEST 3

DIRECTIONS: Each question or incomplete statement is followed by several suggested answers or completions. Select the one that BEST answers the question or completes the statement. *PRINT THE LETTER OF THE CORRECT ANSWER IN THE SPACE AT THE RIGHT.*

1. A notarized document, accompanied by a Certificate of Official Character, is accepted as_____evidence in New York courts.
    A. circumstantial
    B. indirect
    C. hearsay
    D. direct

    1.___

2. The errors and omissions provisions of New York Notary Licensing Law are designed primarily to protect the
    A. notary from criminal liability
    B. parties who receive the notary's services from having a certification invalidated
    C. county of commission, for civil liability
    D. state from civil liability

    2.___

3. A person or business that is put in the place of an original creditor, such as a collection agency, is known as a(n)
    A. assignee
    B. grantee
    C. franchisor
    D. transferent

    3.___

4. A notary public needs to identify a married couple without identification. The best way to do this would be to
    A. have the couple locate another notary public who personally knows them
    B. send them to another notary public who is willing to notarize them without identification
    C. have them bring in a relative, whom the notary does not know, to vouch for them
    D. have them each serve as a credible witness for the other

    4.___

5. The common-law synonym for personal property is
    A. tangibles
    B. chattel
    C. equity
    D. fixtures

    5.___

81

6. The simplest form in which an oath may be lawfully administered is
   A. Do you attest that the contents of this affidavit are true to the best of your knowledge?
   B. Do you solemnly swear that the contents of this affidavit subscribed by you are correct and true?
   C. Do you, the affiant, being of sound mind, solemnly, sincerely, and truly declare that the contents of the affidavit herein are given freely, without compulsion or deceit, and that you are the person whose signature appears herein, so help you God?
   D. The undersigned being warned that willful false statements and the like are punishable by fine or imprisonment, or both, and that such willful false statements and the like may jeopardize the validity of the application or document or any registration resulting therefrom, declares that all statements made of his/her own knowledge are true; and all statements made on information and belief are believed to be true.

7. Felicia Torres, a notary public, marries Fred Compton during her term of office. She elects to take "Felicia Torres Compton" as her married name. For the remainder of her current term in office, she could, when using her name in her notarial capacity, sign her name

   I. "Felicia Torres" until the term expires, and then apply for reappointment under her married name
   II. "Felicia Torres Compton"
   III. "Felicia Torres," and then add her married name in parentheses
   IV. "Mrs. Fred Compton"

   A. I only
   B. I or III
   C. II, III or IV
   D. I, II, III or IV

8. A person's confirmation to a notary that he or she signed a document is a(n)
   A. acknowledgement
   B. certification
   C. attestation
   D. affidavit

9. Under New York Law, a notary who knowingly issues a certificate that contains a false statement or false information is guilty of a
   A. Class A misdemeanor
   B. Class C misdemeanor
   C. Class C felony
   D. Class E felony

10. A notary public's primary responsibility is to verify
    A. that a signer is authorized to sign a document
    B. a signer's identity before notarizing a signature
    C. that a signer is aware of the obligations incurred by signing a document
    D. the validity or legality of the document being signed

11. In issuing a _____, a court decrees that a specified sum of money must be paid to a certain party.

    A. judgement
    B. writ
    C. inquest
    D. endorsement

12. An applicant to the office of notary public in New York was convicted, 11 years ago, of the possession of narcotics. The applicant

    A. cannot be appointed a notary public
    B. can be appointed as a notary public, because the conviction is more than 10 years old
    C. can only be appointed if the conviction was in a state other than New York
    D. can be appointed if the terms of her sentencing have been satisfied completely and she has received a certificate of good conduct from the parole board

13. What is the term for a person who signs ownership interest over to another party?

    A. Co-signer
    B. Endorser
    C. Garnishee
    D. Co-maker

14. Which of the following is NOT required to be an element of a certificate of acknowledgement?

    A. Method used to verify signer ID
    B. Embossed notary seal
    C. Jurisdiction where the document is signed
    D. Venue

15. A notary public, in the second year of his office, moves to another county in New York. The fee charged by the state for changing the address on the commission is the same as the fee that would be charged for

    A. applying for reappointment to the office of notary public
    B. issuing a duplicate identification card for one lost, destroyed or damaged
    C. applying for an initial appointment to the office of notary public
    D. receiving a copy, with a seal, of a certificate of official character from the county clerk

16. A person who has a right to use a portion of a fund, such as an individual retirement fund, is described as

    A. greenlighted
    B. vested
    C. concluded
    D. privileged

17. A New York notary may protest for the non-payment of

    I. Bills of Exchange
    II. Promissory Notes
    III. Checks
    IV. Letters of credit

A. I and II
B. I, II and III
C. II and III
D. I, II, III and IV

18. _____ is the broad term used for any asset that guarantees the repayment of a loan.

    A. Fixture
    B. Collateral
    C. Garnishment
    D. Chattel

19. In order for a mortgage to be acceptable to a county recording officer, the mortgage must be

    A. embossed with a notary seal
    B. acknowledged
    C. witnessed
    D. embossed with the State Seal of New York

20. The wording:

    before me came_____, to me known to be the individual described in and who executed the foregoing instrument and acknowledged that he executed the same.

    is part of the formal declaration known as a(n)

    A. affirmation
    B. affidavit
    C. oath
    D. acknowledgement

21. Frank, a New York notary, MAY lawfully protest a negotiable instrument owned by Glaxon Corporation if he is a(n)

    I. employee of Glaxon without interest in the document
    II. individual party to the protest
    III. stockholder in Glaxon
    IV. executive officer of Glaxon

    A. I only
    B. I or II
    C. II or IV
    D. I, II, III or IV

22. With a_____, a borrower promises to repay the holder of a mortgage.

    A. promissory note
    B. mortgage
    C. truth in lending clause
    D. mortgage insurance policy

23. A_____ will and testament is one written entirely in the handwriting of the person who made the will.
    A. holographic
    B. elective
    C. living
    D. autographic

24. The person who authorizes a power of attorney is known as the
    A. attorney-in-fact
    B. principal
    C. administrator
    D. agent

25. Below his or her signature on a document, a notary public is required to print, typewrite, or stamp
    I.   the words "Notary Public of the State of New York"
    II. his or her name
    III. the name of the county in which he or she originally qualified
    IV. the date upon which his or her commission expires

    A. I only
    B. I and II
    C. I, II and III
    D. I, II, III and IV

KEY (CORRECT ANSWERS)

1. D	6. B	11. A	16. B	21. A
2. B	7. B	12. A	17. D	22. A
3. A	8. A	13. B	18. B	23. A
4. A	9. D	14. B	19. B	24. B
5. B	10. B	15. B	20. D	25. D

EXAMINATION SECTION
TEST 1

DIRECTIONS: Each question or incomplete statement is followed by several suggested answers or completions. Select the one that BEST answers the question or completes the statement. *PRINT THE LETTER OF THE CORRECT ANSWER IN THE SPACE AT THE RIGHT.*

Questions 1-50.

DIRECTIONS: Each of Questions 1 through 50 consists of a word in capital letters followed by four suggested meanings of the word. For each question, choose the word or phrase which means MOST NEARLY the same as the word in capital letters.

1. ABUT
    A. abandon   B. assist   C. border on   D. renounce

2. ABSCOND
    A. draw in   B. give up
    C. refrain from   D. deal off

3. BEQUEATH
    A. deaden   B. hand down   C. make sad   D. scold

4. BOGUS
    A. sad   B. false   C. shocking   D. stolen

5. CALAMITY
    A. disaster   B. female   C. insanity   D. patriot

6. COMPULSORY
    A. binding   B. ordinary   C. protected   D. ruling

7. CONSIGN
    A. agree with   B. benefit
    C. commit   D. drive down

8. DEBILITY
    A. failure   B. legality
    C. quality   D. weakness

9. DEFRAUD
    A. cheat   B. deny
    C. reveal   D. tie

10. DEPOSITION
    A. absence   B. publication
    C. removal   D. testimony

11. DOMICILE
    A. anger   B. dwelling
    C. tame   D. willing

12. HEARSAY
    A. selfish   B. serious   C. rumor   D. unlikely

13. HOMOGENEOUS
    A. human   B. racial   C. similar   D. unwise

14. ILLICIT
    A. understood   B. uneven   C. unkind   D. unlawful

15. LEDGER
    A. book of accounts   B. editor
    C. periodical   D. shelf

16. NARRATIVE
    A. gossip   B. natural   C. negative   D. story

17. PLAUSIBLE
    A. reasonable   B. respectful   C. responsible   D. rightful

18. RECIPIENT
    A. absentee   B. receiver   C. speaker   D. substitute

19. SUBSTANTIATE
    A. appear for   B. arrange
    C. confirm   D. combine

20. SURMISE
    A. aim   B. break   C. guess   D. order

21. ALTER EGO
    A. business partner   B. confidential friend
    C. guide   D. subconscious conflict

22. FOURTH ESTATE
    A. the aristocracy   B. the clergy
    C. the judiciary   D. the newspapers

23. IMPEACH
    A. accuse   B. find guilty
    C. remove   D. try

24. PROPENSITY
    A. dislike   B. helpfulness
    C. inclination   D. supervision

25. SPLENETIC
    A. charming   B. peevish   C. shining   D. sluggish

26. SUBORN
    A. bribe someone to commit perjury
    B. demote someone several levels in rank
    C. deride
    D. substitute

27. TALISMAN
    A. charm   B. juror
    C. prayer shawl D. native

28. VITREOUS
    A. corroding   B. glassy
    C. nourishing   D. sticky

29. WRY
    A. comic   B. grained   C. resilient   D. twisted

30. SIGNATORY
    A. lawyer who draws up a legal document
    B. document that must be signed by a judge
    C. person who signs a document
    D. true copy of a signature

31. RETAINER
    A. fee paid to a lawyer for his services
    B. document held by a third party
    C. court decision to send a prisoner back to custody pending trial
    D. legal requirement to keep certain types of files

32. BEQUEATH
    A. to receive assistance from a charitable organization
    B. to give personal property by will to another
    C. to transfer real property from one person to another
    D. to receive an inheritance upon the death of a relative

33. RATIFY
    A. approve and sanction   B. forego
    C. produce evidence   D. summarize

34. CODICIL
    A. document introduced in evidence in a civil action
    B. subsection of a law
    C. type of legal action that can be brought by a plaintiff
    D. supplement or an addition to a will

35. ALIAS
    A. assumed name   B. in favor of   C. against   D. a writ

36. PROXY
    A. a phony document in a real estate transaction
    B. an opinion by a judge of a civil court
    C. a document containing appointment of an agent
    D. a summons in a lawsuit

37. ALLEGED
    A. innocent   B. asserted   C. guilty   D. called upon

38. EXECUTE
    A. to complete a legal document by signing it
    B. to set requirements
    C. to render services to a duly elected executive of a municipality
    D. to initiate legal action such as a lawsuit

39. NOTARY PUBLIC
    A. lawyer who is running for public office
    B. judge who hears minor cases
    C. public officer, one of whose functions is to administer oaths
    D. lawyer who gives free legal services to persons unable to pay

40. WAIVE
    A. to disturb a calm state of affairs
    B. to knowingly renounce a right or claim
    C. to pardon someone for a minor fault
    D. to purposely mislead a person during an investigation

41. ARRAIGN
    A. to prevent an escape
    B. to defend a prisoner
    C. to verify a document
    D. to accuse in a court of law

42. VOLUNTARY
    A. by free choice   B. necessary
    C. important   D. by design

43. INJUNCTION
    A. act of prohibiting   B. process of inserting
    C. means of arbitrating D. freedom of action

44. AMICABLE
    A. compelled   B. friendly
    C. unimportant   D. insignificant

45. CLOSED SHOP
    A. one that employs only members of a union
    B. one that employs union members and unaffiliated employees
    C. one that employs only employees with previous experience
    D. one that employs skilled and unskilled workers

46. ABDUCT
    A. lead   B. kidnap   C. sudden   D. worthless

47. BIAS
    A. ability   B. envy   C. prejudice   D. privilege

48. COERCE
    A. cancel   B. force   C. rescind   D. rugged

49. CONDONE 49.____
 A. combine B. pardon C. revive D. spice
50. CONSISTENCY 50.____
 A. bravery B. readiness
 C. strain D. uniformity

KEY (CORRECT ANSWERS)

1. C	11. B	21. B	31. A	41. D
2. D	12. C	22. D	32. B	42. A
3. B	13. C	23. A	33. A	43. A
4. B	14. D	24. C	34. D	44. B
5. A	15. A	25. B	35. A	45. A
6. A	16. D	26. A	36. C	46. B
7. C	17. A	27. A	37. B	47. C
8. D	18. B	28. B	38. A	48. B
9. A	19. C	29. D	39. C	49. B
10. D	20. C	30. C	40. B	50. D

TEST 2

DIRECTIONS: Each question or incomplete statement is followed by several suggested answers or completions. Select the one that BEST answers the question or completes the statement. *PRINT THE LETTER OF THE CORRECT ANSWER IN THE SPACE AT THE RIGHT.*

1. In the sentence, *The prisoner was fractious when brought to the station house*, the word *fractious* means MOST NEARLY
   A. penitent
   B. talkative
   C. irascible
   D. broken-hearted

   1.____

2. In the sentence, *The judge was implacable when the attorney pleaded for leniency*, the word *implacable* means MOST NEARLY
   A. inexorable
   B. disinterested
   C. inattentive
   D. indifferent

   2.____

3. In the sentence, *The court ordered the mendacious statements stricken from the record*, the word *mendacious* means MOST NEARLY
   A. begging
   B. lying
   C. threatening
   D. lengthy

   3.____

4. In the sentence, *The district attorney spoke in a strident voice*, the word *strident* means MOST NEARLY
   A. loud
   B. harsh-sounding
   C. sing-song
   D. low

   4.____

5. In the sentence, *The speaker had a predilection for long sentences*, the word *predilection* means MOST NEARLY
   A. aversion
   B. talent
   C. propensity
   D. diffidence

   5.____

6. A person who has an uncontrollable desire to steal without need is called a
   A. dipsomaniac
   B. kleptomaniac
   C. monomaniac
   D. pyromaniac

   6.____

7. In the sentence, *Malice was immanent in all his remarks*, the word *immanent* means MOST NEARLY
   A. elevated
   B. inherent
   C. threatening
   D. foreign

   7.____

8. In the sentence, *The extant copies of the document were found in the safe*, the word *extant* means MOST NEARLY
   A. existing
   B. original
   C. forged
   D. duplicate

   8.____

9. In the sentence, *The recruit was more complaisant after the captain spoke to him*, the word *complaisant* means MOST NEARLY
   A. calm
   B. affable
   C. irritable
   D. confident

   9.____

10. In the sentence, *The man was captured under highly creditable circumstances*, the word *creditable* means MOST NEARLY

   A. doubtful
   B. believable
   C. praiseworthy
   D. unexpected

11. In the sentence, *His superior officers were more sagacious than he*, the word *sagacious* means MOST NEARLY

   A. shrewd
   B. obtuse
   C. absurd
   D. verbose

12. In the sentence, *He spoke with impunity*, the word *impunity* means MOST NEARLY

   A. rashness
   B. caution
   C. without fear
   D. immunity

13. In the sentence, *The new officer displayed unusual temerity during the emergency*, the word *temerity* means MOST NEARLY

   A. fear
   B. rashness
   C. calmness
   D. anxiety

14. In the sentence, *The portions of food were parsimoniously served*, the word *parsimoniously* means MOST NEARLY

   A. stingily
   B. piously
   C. elaborately
   D. generously

15. In the sentence, *Generally the speaker's remarks were sententious*, the word *sententious* means MOST NEARLY

   A. verbose
   B. witty
   C. argumentative
   D. pithy

Questions 16-20.

DIRECTIONS: Next to the number which corresponds with the number of each item in Column I, place the letter preceding the adjective in Column II which BEST describes the persons in Column I.

COLUMN I		COLUMN II
16. Talkative woman	A.	abstemious
17. Person on a reducing diet	B.	pompous
18. Scholarly professor	C.	erudite
19. Man who seldom speaks	D.	benevolent
20. Charitable person	E.	docile
	F.	loquacious
	G.	indefatigable
	H.	taciturn

Questions 21-25.

DIRECTIONS: Next to the number which corresponds with the number preceding each profession in Column I, place the letter preceding the word in Column II which BEST explains the subject matter of that profession.

COLUMN I	COLUMN II	
21. Geologist	A. animals	21.
22. Oculist	B. eyes	22.
23. Podiatrist	C. feet	23.
24. Palmist	D. fortune-telling	24.
25. Zoologist	E. language	25.
	F. rocks	
	G. stamps	
	H. woman	

Questions 26-30.

DIRECTIONS: Next to the number corresponding to the number of each of the words in Column I, place the letter preceding the word in Column II that is MOST NEARLY OPPOSITE to it in meaning.

COLUMN I	COLUMN II	
26. comely	A. beautiful	26.
27. eminent	B. cowardly	27.
28. frugal	C. kind	28.
29. gullible	D. sedate	29.
30. valiant	E. shrewd	30.
	F. ugly	
	G. unknown	
	H. wasteful	

KEY (CORRECT ANSWERS)

1. C	11. A	21. F
2. A	12. D	22. B
3. B	13. B	23. C
4. B	14. A	24. D
5. C	15. D	25. A
6. B	16. F	26. F
7. B	17. A	27. G
8. A	18. C	28. H
9. B	19. H	29. E
10. C	20. D	30. B

EXAMINATION SECTION
TEST 1

DIRECTIONS: Each question or incomplete statement is followed by several suggested answers or completions. Select the one that BEST answers the question or completes the statement. *PRINT THE LETTER OF THE CORRECT ANSWER IN THE SPACE AT THE RIGHT.*

Questions 1-25.

DIRECTIONS: In each of Questions 1 through 25, select the lettered word or phrase which means MOST NEARLY the same as the capitalized word.

1. INTERROGATE
   A. question   B. arrest   C. search   D. rebuff

2. PERVERSE
   A. manageable   B. poetic
   C. contrary   D. patient

3. ADVOCATE
   A. champion   B. employ
   C. select   D. advise

4. APPARENT
   A. desirable   B. clear
   C. partial   D. possible

5. INSINUATE
   A. survey   B. strengthen
   C. suggest   D. insist

6. MOMENTOUS
   A. important   B. immediate   C. delayed   D. short

7. AUXILIARY
   A. exciting   B. assisting   C. upsetting   D. available

8. ADMONISH
   A. praise   B. increase   C. warn   D. polish

9. ANTICIPATE
   A. agree   B. expect   C. conceal   D. approve

10. APPREHEND
    A. confuse   B. sentence   C. release   D. seize

11. CLEMENCY
    A. silence   B. freedom   C. mercy   D. severity

12. THWART
    A. enrage   B. strike   C. choke   D. block

13. RELINQUISH
    A. stretch   B. give up   C. weaken   D. flee from
14. CURTAIL
    A. stop   B. reduce   C. repair   D. insult
15. INACCESSIBLE
    A. obstinate   B. unreachable
    C. unreasonable   D. puzzling
16. PERTINENT
    A. related   B. saucy   C. durable   D. impatient
17. INTIMIDATE
    A. encourage   B. hunt   C. beat   D. frighten
18. INTEGRITY
    A. honesty   B. wisdom
    C. understanding   D. persistence
19. UTILIZE
    A. use   B. manufacture
    C. help   D. include
20. SUPPLEMENT
    A. regulate   B. demand   C. add   D. answer
21. INDISPENSABLE
    A. essential   B. neglected
    C. truthful   D. unnecessary
22. ATTAIN
    A. introduce   B. spoil   C. achieve   D. study
23. PRECEDE
    A. break away   B. go ahead
    C. begin   D. come before
24. HAZARD
    A. penalty   B. adventure   C. handicap   D. danger
25. DETRIMENTAL
    A. uncertain   B. harmful   C. fierce   D. horrible

KEY (CORRECT ANSWERS)

1. A	6. A	11. C	16. A	21. A
2. C	7. B	12. D	17. D	22. C
3. A	8. C	13. B	18. A	23. D
4. B	9. B	14. B	19. A	24. D
5. C	10. D	15. B	20. C	25. B

TEST 2

DIRECTIONS: Each question or incomplete statement is followed by several suggested answers or completions. Select the one that BEST answers the question or completes the statement. *PRINT THE LETTER OF THE CORRECT ANSWER IN THE SPACE AT THE RIGHT.*

Questions 1-20.

DIRECTIONS: In each of Questions 1 through 20, select the lettered word or phrase which means MOST NEARLY the same as the capitalized word.

1. IMPLY
    - A. agree to
    - B. hint at
    - C. laugh at
    - D. mimic
    - E. reduce

2. APPRAISAL
    - A. allowance
    - B. composition
    - C. prohibition
    - D. quantity
    - E. valuation

3. DISBURSE
    - A. approve
    - B. expend
    - C. prevent
    - D. relay
    - E. restrict

4. POSTERITY
    - A. back payment
    - B. current procedure
    - C. final effort
    - D. future generations
    - E. rare specimen

5. PUNCTUAL
    - A. clear
    - B. honest
    - C. polite
    - D. prompt
    - E. prudent

6. PRECARIOUS
    - A. abundant
    - B. alarmed
    - C. cautious
    - D. insecure
    - E. placid

7. FOSTER
    - A. delegate
    - B. demote
    - C. encourage
    - D. plead
    - E. surround

8. PINNACLE
    - A. center
    - B. crisis
    - C. outcome
    - D. peak
    - E. personification

9. COMPONENT
    - A. flattery
    - B. opposite
    - C. part
    - D. revision
    - E. trend

10. SOLICIT
    - A. ask
    - B. prohibit
    - C. promise
    - D. revoke
    - E. surprise

11. LIAISON 11.___
   A. asset   B. coordination   C. difference
   D. policy   E. procedure

12. ALLEGE 12.___
   A. assert   B. break   C. irritate
   D. reduce   E. wait

13. INFILTRATION 13.___
   A. consumption   B. disposal   C. enforcement
   D. penetration   E. seizure

14. SALVAGE 14.___
   A. announce   B. combine   C. prolong
   D. save   E. try

15. MOTIVE 15.___
   A. attack   B. favor   C. incentive
   D. patience   E. tribute

16. PROVOKE 16.___
   A. adjust   B. incite   C. leave
   D. obtain   E. practice

17. SURGE 17.___
   A. branch   B. contract   C. revenge
   D. rush   E. want

18. MAGNIFY 18.___
   A. attract   B. demand   C. generate
   D. increase   E. puzzle

19. PREPONDERANCE 19.___
   A. decision   B. judgment   C. outweighing
   D. submission   E. warning

20. ABATE 20.___
   A. assist   B. coerce   C. diminish
   D. indulge   E. trade

Questions 21-30.

DIRECTIONS: In each of Questions 21 through 30, select the lettered word or phrase which means MOST NEARLY, the same as, or the opposite of, the capitalized word.

21. VINDICTIVE 21.___
   A. centrifugal   B. forgiving   C. molten
   D. tedious   E. vivacious

22. SCOPE 22.___
   A. compact   B. detriment   C. facsimile
   D. potable   E. range

23. HINDER
    A. amplify   B. aver   C. method
    D. observe   E. retard
    23.___

24. IRATE
    A. adhere   B. angry   C. authentic
    D. peremptory   E. vacillate
    24.___

25. APATHY
    A. accessory   B. availability   C. fervor
    D. pacify   E. stride
    25.___

26. LUCRATIVE
    A. effective   B. imperfect   C. injurious
    D. timely   E. worthless
    26.___

27. DIVERSITY
    A. convection   B. slip   C. temerity
    D. uniformity   E. viscosity
    27.___

28. OVERT
    A. laugh   B. lighter   C. orifice
    D. quay   E. sly
    28.___

29. SPORADIC
    A. divide   B. incumbrance   C. livid
    D. occasional   E. original
    29.___

30. PREVARICATE
    A. hesitate   B. increase   C. lie
    D. procrastinate   E. reject
    30.___

KEY (CORRECT ANSWERS)

1.	B	11.	B	21.	B
2.	E	12.	A	22.	E
3.	B	13.	D	23.	E
4.	D	14.	D	24.	B
5.	D	15.	C	25.	C
6.	D	16.	B	26.	E
7.	C	17.	D	27.	D
8.	D	18.	D	28.	E
9.	C	19.	C	29.	D
10.	A	20.	C	30.	C

TEST 3

DIRECTIONS: Each question or incomplete statement is followed by several suggested answers or completions. Select the one that BEST answers the question or completes the statement. *PRINT THE LETTER OF THE CORRECT ANSWER IN THE SPACE AT THE RIGHT.*

Questions 1-30.

DIRECTIONS: In each of Questions 1 through 30, select the lettered word which means MOST NEARLY the same as the capitalized word.

1. AVARICE
   A. flight   B. greed   C. pride   D. thrift

2. PREDATORY
   A. offensive   B. plundering
   C. previous   D. timeless

3. VINDICATE
   A. clear   B. conquer   C. correct   D. illustrate

4. INVETERATE
   A. backward   B. erect   C. habitual   D. lucky

5. DISCERN
   A. describe   B. fabricate   C. recognize   D. seek

6. COMPLACENT
   A. indulgent   B. listless   C. overjoyed   D. satisfied

7. ILLICIT
   A. insecure   B. unclear   C. unlawful   D. unlimited

8. PROCRASTINATE
   A. declare   B. multiply   C. postpone   D. steal

9. IMPASSIVE
   A. calm   B. frustrated
   C. thoughtful   D. unhappy

10. AMICABLE
    A. cheerful   B. flexible
    C. friendly   D. poised

11. FEASIBLE
    A. breakable   B. easy
    C. likeable   D. practicable

12. INNOCUOUS
    A. harmless   B. insecure
    C. insincere   D. unfavorable

13. OSTENSIBLE
    A. apparent B. hesitant C. reluctant D. showy 13.___
14. INDOMITABLE
    A. excessive B. unconquerable
    C. unreasonable D. unthinkable 14.___
15. CRAVEN
    A. cowardly B. hidden C. miserly D. needed 15.___
16. ALLAY
    A. discuss B. quiet C. refine D. remove 16.___
17. ALLUDE
    A. denounce B. refer C. state D. support 17.___
18. NEGLIGENCE
    A. carelessness B. denial
    C. objection D. refusal 18.___
19. AMEND
    A. correct B. destroy C. end D. list 19.___
20. RELEVANT
    A. conclusive B. careful
    C. obvious D. related 20.___
21. VERIFY
    A. challenge B. change C. confirm D. reveal 21.___
22. INSIGNIFICANT
    A. incorrect B. limited
    C. unimportant D. undesirable 22.___
23. RESCIND
    A. annul B. deride C. extol D. indulge 23.___
24. AUGMENT
    A. alter B. increase C. obey D. perceive 24.___
25. AUTONOMOUS
    A. conceptual B. constant
    C. defamatory D. independent 25.___
26. TRANSCRIPT
    A. copy B. report C. sentence D. termination 26.___
27. DISCORDANT
    A. quarrelsome B. comprised
    C. effusive D. harmonious 27.___
28. DISTEND
    A. constrict B. dilate C. redeem D. silence 28.___

29. EMANATE
   A. bridge   B. coherency   C. conquer   D. flow

30. EXULTANT
   A. easily upset   B. in high spirits
   C. subject to moods   D. very much over-priced

KEY (CORRECT ANSWERS)

1. B	11. D	21. C
2. B	12. A	22. C
3. A	13. A	23. A
4. C	14. B	24. B
5. C	15. A	25. D
6. D	16. B	26. A
7. C	17. B	27. A
8. C	18. A	28. B
9. A	19. A	29. D
10. C	20. D	30. B

GLOSSARY OF LEGAL TERMS

TABLE OF CONTENTS

	Page
Action ... Affiant	1
Affidavit ... At Bar	2
At Issue ... Burden of Proof	3
Business ... Commute	4
Complainant ... Conviction	5
Cooperative ... Demur (v.)	6
Demurrage ... Endorsement	7
Enjoin ... Facsimile	8
Factor ... Guilty	9
Habeas Corpus ... Incumbrance	10
Indemnify ... Laches	11
Landlord and Tenant ... Malice	12
Mandamus ... Obiter Dictum	13
Object (v.) ... Perjury	14
Perpetuity ... Proclamation	15
Proffered Evidence ... Referee	16
Referendum ... Stare Decisis	17
State ... Term	18
Testamentary ... Warrant (Warranty) (v.)	19
Warrant (n.) ... Zoning	20

GLOSSARY OF LEGAL TERMS

A

ACTION - "Action" includes a civil action and a criminal action.

A FORTIORI - A term meaning you can reason one thing from the existence of certain facts.

A POSTERIORI - From what goes after; from effect to cause.

A PRIORI - From what goes before; from cause to effect.

AB INITIO - From the beginning.

ABATE - To diminish or put an end to.

ABET - To encourage the commission of a crime.

ABEYANCE - Suspension, temporary suppression.

ABIDE - To accept the consequences of.

ABJURE - To renounce; give up.

ABRIDGE - To reduce; contract; diminish.

ABROGATE - To annul, repeal, or destroy.

ABSCOND - To hide or absent oneself to avoid legal action.

ABSTRACT - A summary.

ABUT - To border on, to touch.

ACCESS - Approach; in real property law it means the right of the owner of property to the use of the highway or road next to his land, without obstruction by intervening property owners.

ACCESSORY - In criminal law, it means the person who contributes or aids in the commission of a crime.

ACCOMMODATED PARTY - One to whom credit is extended on the strength of another person signing a commercial paper.

ACCOMMODATION PAPER - A commercial paper to which the accommodating party has put his name.

ACCOMPLICE - In criminal law, it means a person who together with the principal offender commits a crime.

ACCORD - An agreement to accept something different or less than that to which one is entitled, which extinguishes the entire obligation.

ACCOUNT - A statement of mutual demands in the nature of debt and credit between parties.

ACCRETION - The act of adding to a thing; in real property law, it means gradual accumulation of land by natural causes.

ACCRUE - To grow to; to be added to.

ACKNOWLEDGMENT - The act of going before an official authorized to take acknowledgments, and acknowledging an act as one's own.

ACQUIESCENCE - A silent appearance of consent.

ACQUIT - To legally determine the innocence of one charged with a crime.

AD INFINITUM - Indefinitely.

AD LITEM - For the suit.

AD VALOREM - According to value.

ADJECTIVE LAW - Rules of procedure.

ADJUDICATION - The judgment given in a case.

ADMIRALTY - Court having jurisdiction over maritime cases.

ADULT - Sixteen years old or over (in criminal law).

ADVANCE - In commercial law, it means to pay money or render other value before it is due.

ADVERSE - Opposed; contrary.

ADVOCATE - (v.) To speak in favor of;
(n.) One who assists, defends, or pleads for another.

AFFIANT - A person who makes and signs an affidavit.

AFFIDAVIT - A written and sworn to declaration of facts, voluntarily made.
AFFINITY- The relationship between persons through marriage with the kindred of each other; distinguished from consanguinity, which is the relationship by blood.
AFFIRM - To ratify; also when an appellate court affirms a judgment, decree, or order, it means that it is valid and right and must stand as rendered in the lower court.
AFOREMENTIONED; AFORESAID - Before or already said.
AGENT - One who represents and acts for another.
AID AND COMFORT - To help; encourage.
ALIAS - A name not one's true name.
ALIBI - A claim of not being present at a certain place at a certain time.
ALLEGE - To assert.
ALLOTMENT - A share or portion.
AMBIGUITY - Uncertainty; capable of being understood in more than one way.
AMENDMENT - Any language made or proposed as a change in some principal writing.
AMICUS CURIAE - A friend of the court; one who has an interest in a case, although not a party in the case, who volunteers advice upon matters of law to the judge. For example, a brief amicus curiae.
AMORTIZATION - To provide for a gradual extinction of (a future obligation) in advance of maturity, especially, by periodical contributions to a sinking fund which will be adequate to discharge a debt or make a replacement when it becomes necessary.
ANCILLARY - Aiding, auxiliary.
ANNOTATION - A note added by way of comment or explanation.
ANSWER - A written statement made by a defendant setting forth the grounds of his defense.
ANTE - Before.
ANTE MORTEM - Before death.
APPEAL - The removal of a case from a lower court to one of superior jurisdiction for the purpose of obtaining a review.
APPEARANCE - Coming into court as a party to a suit.
APPELLANT - The party who takes an appeal from one court or jurisdiction to another (appellate) court for review.
APPELLEE - The party against whom an appeal is taken.
APPROPRIATE - To make a thing one's own.
APPROPRIATION - Prescribing the destination of a thing; the act of the legislature designating a particular fund, to be applied to some object of government expenditure.
APPURTENANT - Belonging to; accessory or incident to.
ARBITER - One who decides a dispute; a referee.
ARBITRARY - Unreasoned; not governed by any fixed rules or standard.
ARGUENDO - By way of argument.
ARRAIGN - To call the prisoner before the court to answer to a charge.
ASSENT - A declaration of willingness to do something in compliance with a request.
ASSERT - Declare.
ASSESS - To fix the rate or amount.
ASSIGN - To transfer; to appoint; to select for a particular purpose.
ASSIGNEE - One who receives an assignment.
ASSIGNOR - One who makes an assignment.
AT BAR - Before the court.

AT ISSUE - When parties in an action come to a point where one asserts something and the other denies it.
ATTACH - Seize property by court order and sometimes arrest a person.
ATTEST - To witness a will, etc.; act of attestation.
AVERMENT - A positive statement of facts.

B

BAIL - To obtain the release of a person from legal custody by giving security and promising that he shall appear in court; to deliver (goods, etc.) in trust to a person for a special purpose.
BAILEE - One to whom personal property is delivered under a contract of bailment.
BAILMENT - Delivery of personal property to another to be held for a certain purpose and to be returned when the purpose is accomplished.
BAILOR - The party who delivers goods to another, under a contract of bailment.
BANC (OR BANK) - Bench; the place where a court sits permanently or regularly; also the assembly of all the judges of a court.
BANKRUPT - An insolvent person, technically, one declared to be bankrupt after a bankruptcy proceeding.
BAR - The legal profession.
BARRATRY - Exciting groundless judicial proceedings.
BARTER - A contract by which parties exchange goods for other goods.
BATTERY - Illegal interfering with another's person.
BEARER - In commercial law, it means the person in possession of a commercial paper which is payable to the bearer.
BENCH - The court itself or the judge.
BENEFICIARY - A person benefiting under a will, trust, or agreement.
BEST EVIDENCE RULE, THE - Except as otherwise provided by statute, no evidence other than the writing itself is admissible to prove the content of a writing. This section shall be known and may be cited as the best evidence rule.
BEQUEST - A gift of personal property under a will.
BILL - A formal written statement of complaint to a court of justice; also, a draft of an act of the legislature before it becomes a law; also, accounts for goods sold, services rendered, or work done.
BONA FIDE - In or with good faith; honestly.
BOND - An instrument by which the maker promises to pay a sum of money to another, usually providing that upon performances of a certain condition the obligation shall be void.
BOYCOTT - A plan to prevent the carrying on of a business by wrongful means.
BREACH - The breaking or violating of a law, or the failure to carry out a duty.
BRIEF - A written document, prepared by a lawyer to serve as the basis of an argument upon a case in court, usually an appellate court.
BURDEN OF PRODUCING EVIDENCE - The obligation of a party to introduce evidence sufficient to avoid a ruling against him on the issue.
BURDEN OF PROOF - The obligation of a party to establish by evidence a requisite degree of belief concerning a fact in the mind of the trier of fact or the court. The burden of proof may require a party to raise a reasonable doubt concerning the existence of nonexistence of a fact or that he establish the existence or nonexistence of a fact by a preponderance of the evidence, by clear and convincing proof, or by proof beyond a reasonable doubt.

Except as otherwise provided by law, the burden of proof requires proof by a preponderance of the evidence.

BUSINESS, A - Shall include every kind of business, profession, occupation, calling or operation of institutions, whether carried on for profit or not.

BY-LAWS - Regulations, ordinances, or rules enacted by a corporation, association, etc., for its own government.

C

CANON - A doctrine; also, a law or rule, of a church or association in particular.

CAPIAS - An order to arrest.

CAPTION - In a pleading, deposition or other paper connected with a case in court, it is the heading or introductory clause which shows the names of the parties, name of the court, number of the case on the docket or calendar, etc.

CARRIER - A person or corporation undertaking to transport persons or property.

CASE - A general term for an action, cause, suit, or controversy before a judicial body.

CAUSE - A suit, litigation or action before a court.

CAVEAT EMPTOR - Let the buyer beware. This term expresses the rule that the purchaser of an article must examine, judge, and test it for himself, being bound to discover any obvious defects or imperfections.

CERTIFICATE - A written representation that some legal formality has been complied with.

CERTIORARI - To be informed of; the name of a writ issued by a superior court directing the lower court to send up to the former the record and proceedings of a case.

CHANGE OF VENUE - To remove place of trial from one place to another.

CHARGE - An obligation or duty; a formal complaint; an instruction of the court to the jury upon a case.

CHARTER - (n.) The authority by virtue of which an organized body acts;
(v.) in mercantile law, it means to hire or lease a vehicle or vessel for transportation.

CHATTEL - An article of personal property.

CHATTEL MORTGAGE - A mortgage on personal property.

CIRCUIT - A division of the country, for the administration of justice; a geographical area served by a court.

CITATION - The act of the court by which a person is summoned or cited; also, a reference to legal authority.

CIVIL (ACTIONS)- It indicates the private rights and remedies of individuals in contrast to the word "criminal" (actions) which relates to prosecution for violation of laws.

CLAIM (n.) - Any demand held or asserted as of right.

CODICIL - An addition to a will.

CODIFY - To arrange the laws of a country into a code.

COGNIZANCE - Notice or knowledge.

COLLATERAL - By the side; accompanying; an article or thing given to secure performance of a promise.

COMITY - Courtesy; the practice by which one court follows the decision of another court on the same question.

COMMIT - To perform, as an act; to perpetrate, as a crime; to send a person to prison.

COMMON LAW - As distinguished from law created by the enactment of the legislature (called statutory law), it relates to those principles and rules of action which derive their authority solely from usages and customs of immemorial antiquity, particularly with reference to the ancient unwritten law of England. The written pronouncements of the common law are found in court decisions.

COMMUTE - Change punishment to one less severe.

COMPLAINANT - One who applies to the court for legal redress.
COMPLAINT - The pleading of a plaintiff in a civil action; or a charge that a person has committed a specified offense.
COMPROMISE - An arrangement for settling a dispute by agreement.
CONCUR - To agree, consent.
CONCURRENT - Running together, at the same time.
CONDEMNATION - Taking private property for public use on payment therefor.
CONDITION - Mode or state of being; a qualification or restriction.
CONDUCT - Active and passive behavior; both verbal and nonverbal.
CONFESSION - Voluntary statement of guilt of crime.
CONFIDENTIAL COMMUNICATION BETWEEN CLIENT AND LAWYER - Information transmitted between a client and his lawyer in the course of that relationship and in confidence by a means which, so far as the client is aware, discloses the information to no third persons other than those who are present to further the interest of the client in the consultation or those to whom disclosure is reasonably necessary for the transmission of the information or the accomplishment of the purpose for which the lawyer is consulted, and includes a legal opinion formed and the advice given by the lawyer in the course of that relationship.
CONFRONTATION - Witness testifying in presence of defendant.
CONSANGUINITY - Blood relationship.
CONSIGN - To give in charge; commit; entrust; to send or transmit goods to a merchant, factor, or agent for sale.
CONSIGNEE - One to whom a consignment is made.
CONSIGNOR - One who sends or makes a consignment.
CONSPIRACY - In criminal law, it means an agreement between two or more persons to commit an unlawful act.
CONSPIRATORS - Persons involved in a conspiracy.
CONSTITUTION - The fundamental law of a nation or state.
CONSTRUCTION OF GENDERS - The masculine gender includes the feminine and neuter.
CONSTRUCTION OF SINGULAR AND PLURAL - The singular number includes the plural; and the plural, the singular.
CONSTRUCTION OF TENSES - The present tense includes the past and future tenses; and the future, the present.
CONSTRUCTIVE - An act or condition assumed from other parts or conditions.
CONSTRUE - To ascertain the meaning of language.
CONSUMMATE - To complete.
CONTIGUOUS - Adjoining; touching; bounded by.
CONTINGENT - Possible, but not assured; dependent upon some condition.
CONTINUANCE - The adjournment or postponement of an action pending in a court.
CONTRA - Against, opposed to; contrary.
CONTRACT - An agreement between two or more persons to do or not to do a particular thing.
CONTROVERT - To dispute, deny.
CONVERSION - Dealing with the personal property of another as if it were one's own, without right.
CONVEYANCE - An instrument transferring title to land.
CONVICTION - Generally, the result of a criminal trial which ends in a judgment or sentence that the defendant is guilty as charged.

COOPERATIVE - A cooperative is a voluntary organization of persons with a common interest, formed and operated along democratic lines for the purpose of supplying services at cost to its members and other patrons, who contribute both capital and business.
CORPUS DELICTI - The body of a crime; the crime itself.
CORROBORATE - To strengthen; to add weight by additional evidence.
COUNTERCLAIM - A claim presented by a defendant in opposition to or deduction from the claim of the plaintiff.
COUNTY - Political subdivision of a state.
COVENANT - Agreement.
CREDIBLE - Worthy of belief.
CREDITOR - A person to whom a debt is owing by another person, called the "debtor."
CRIMINAL ACTION - Includes criminal proceedings.
CRIMINAL INFORMATION - Same as complaint.
CRITERION (sing.)
CRITERIA (plural) - A means or tests for judging; a standard or standards.
CROSS-EXAMINATION - Examination of a witness by a party other than the direct examiner upon a matter that is within the scope of the direct examination of the witness.
CULPABLE - Blamable.
CY-PRES - As near as (possible). The rule of *cy-pres* is a rule for the construction of instruments in equity by which the intention of the party is carried out *as near as may be*, when it would be impossible or illegal to give it literal effect.

D

DAMAGES - A monetary compensation, which may be recovered in the courts by any person who has suffered loss, or injury, whether to his person, property or rights through the unlawful act or omission or negligence of another.
DECLARANT - A person who makes a statement.
DE FACTO - In fact; actually but without legal authority.
DE JURE - Of right; legitimate; lawful.
DE MINIMIS - Very small or trifling.
DE NOVO - Anew; afresh; a second time.
DEBT - A specified sum of money owing to one person from another, including not only the obligation of the debtor to pay, but the right of the creditor to receive and enforce payment.
DECEDENT - A dead person.
DECISION - A judgment or decree pronounced by a court in determination of a case.
DECREE - An order of the court, determining the rights of all parties to a suit.
DEED - A writing containing a contract sealed and delivered; particularly to convey real property.
DEFALCATION - Misappropriation of funds.
DEFAMATION - Injuring one's reputation by false statements.
DEFAULT - The failure to fulfill a duty, observe a promise, discharge an obligation, or perform an agreement.
DEFENDANT - The person defending or denying; the party against whom relief or recovery is sought in an action or suit.
DEFRAUD - To practice fraud; to cheat or trick.
DELEGATE (v.)- To entrust to the care or management of another.
DELICTUS - A crime.
DEMUR (v.) - To dispute the sufficiency in law of the pleading of the other side.

DEMURRAGE - In maritime law, it means, the sum fixed or allowed as remuneration to the owners of a ship for the detention of their vessel beyond the number of days allowed for loading and unloading or for sailing; also used in railroad terminology.
DENIAL - A form of pleading; refusing to admit the truth of a statement, charge, etc.
DEPONENT - One who gives testimony under oath reduced to writing.
DEPOSITION - Testimony given under oath outside of court for use in court or for the purpose of obtaining information in preparation for trial of a case.
DETERIORATION - A degeneration such as from decay, corrosion or disintegration.
DETRIMENT - Any loss or harm to person or property.
DEVIATION - A turning aside.
DEVISE - A gift of real property by the last will and testament of the donor.
DICTUM (sing.)
DICTA (plural) - Any statements made by the court in an opinion concerning some rule of law not necessarily involved nor essential to the determination of the case.
DIRECT EVIDENCE - Evidence that directly proves a fact, without an inference or presumption, and which in itself if true, conclusively establishes that fact.
DIRECT EXAMINATION - The first examination of a witness upon a matter that is not within the scope of a previous examination of the witness.
DISAFFIRM - To repudiate.
DISMISS - In an action or suit, it means to dispose of the case without any further consideration or hearing.
DISSENT - To denote disagreement of one or more judges of a court with the decision passed by the majority upon a case before them.
DOCKET (n.) - A formal record, entered in brief, of the proceedings in a court.
DOCTRINE - A rule, principle, theory of law.
DOMICILE - That place where a man has his true, fixed and permanent home to which whenever he is absent he has the intention of returning.
DRAFT (n.) - A commercial paper ordering payment of money drawn by one person on another.
DRAWEE - The person who is requested to pay the money.
DRAWER - The person who draws the commercial paper and addresses it to the drawee.
DUPLICATE - A counterpart produced by the same impression as the original enlargements and miniatures, or by mechanical or electronic re-recording, or by chemical reproduction, or by other equivalent technique which accurately reproduces the original.
DURESS - Use of force to compel performance or non-performance of an act.

E

EASEMENT - A liberty, privilege, or advantage without profit, in the lands of another.
EGRESS - Act or right of going out or leaving; emergence.
EIUSDEM GENERIS - Of the same kind, class or nature. A rule used in the construction of language in a legal document.
EMBEZZLEMENT - To steal; to appropriate fraudulently to one's own use property entrusted to one's care.
EMBRACERY - Unlawful attempt to influence jurors, etc., but not by offering value.
EMINENT DOMAIN - The right of a state to take private property for public use.
ENACT - To make into a law.
ENDORSEMENT - Act of writing one's name on the back of a note, bill or similar written instrument.

ENJOIN - To require a person, by writ of injunction from a court of equity, to perform or to abstain or desist from some act.
ENTIRETY - The whole; that which the law considers as one whole, and not capable of being divided into parts.
ENTRAPMENT - Inducing one to commit a crime so as to arrest him.
ENUMERATED - Mentioned specifically; designated.
ENURE - To operate or take effect.
EQUITY - In its broadest sense, this term denotes the spirit and the habit of fairness, justness, and right dealing which regulate the conduct of men.
ERROR - A mistake of law, or the false or irregular application of law as will nullify the judicial proceedings.
ESCROW - A deed, bond or other written engagement, delivered to a third person, to be delivered by him only upon the performance or fulfillment of some condition.
ESTATE - The interest which any one has in lands, or in any other subject of property.
ESTOP - To stop, bar, or impede.
ESTOPPEL - A rule of law which prevents a man from alleging or denying a fact, because of his own previous act.
ET AL. (alii) - And others.
ET SEQ. (sequential) - And the following.
ET UX. (uxor) - And wife.
EVIDENCE - Testimony, writings, material objects, or other things presented to the senses that are offered to prove the existence or non-existence of a fact.
　　　Means from which inferences may be drawn as a basis of proof in duly constituted judicial or fact finding tribunals, and includes testimony in the form of opinion and hearsay.
EX CONTRACTU
EX DELICTO - In law, rights and causes of action are divided into two classes, those arising *ex contractu* (from a contract) and those arising *ex delicto* (from a delict or tort).
EX OFFICIO - From office; by virtue of the office.
EX PARTE - On one side only; by or for one.
EX POST FACTO - After the fact.
EX POST FACTO LAW - A law passed after an act was done which retroactively makes such act a crime.
EX REL. (relations) - Upon relation or information.
EXCEPTION - An objection upon a matter of law to a decision made, either before or after judgment by a court.
EXECUTOR (male)
EXECUTRIX (female) - A person who has been appointed by will to execute the will.
EXECUTORY - That which is yet to be executed or performed.
EXEMPT - To release from some liability to which others are subject.
EXONERATION - The removal of a burden, charge or duty.
EXTRADITION - Surrender of a fugitive from one nation to another.

F

F.A.S.- "Free alongside ship"; delivery at dock for ship named.
F.O.B.- "Free on board"; seller will deliver to car, truck, vessel, or other conveyance by which goods are to be transported, without expense or risk of loss to the buyer or consignee.
FABRICATE - To construct; to invent a false story.
FACSIMILE - An exact or accurate copy of an original instrument.

FACTOR - A commercial agent.
FEASANCE - The doing of an act.
FELONIOUS - Criminal, malicious.
FELONY - Generally, a criminal offense that may be punished by death or imprisonment for more than one year as differentiated from a misdemeanor.
FEME SOLE - A single woman.
FIDUCIARY - A person who is invested with rights and powers to be exercised for the benefit of another person.
FIERI FACIAS - A writ of execution commanding the sheriff to levy and collect the amount of a judgment from the goods and chattels of the judgment debtor.
FINDING OF FACT - Determination from proof or judicial notice of the existence of a fact. A ruling implies a supporting finding of fact; no separate or formal finding is required unless required by a statute of this state.
FISCAL - Relating to accounts or the management of revenue.
FORECLOSURE (sale) - A sale of mortgaged property to obtain satisfaction of the mortgage out of the sale proceeds.
FORFEITURE - A penalty, a fine.
FORGERY - Fabricating or producing falsely, counterfeited.
FORTUITOUS - Accidental.
FORUM - A court of justice; a place of jurisdiction.
FRAUD - Deception; trickery.
FREEHOLDER - One who owns real property.
FUNGIBLE - Of such kind or nature that one specimen or part may be used in the place of another.

G

GARNISHEE - Person garnished.
GARNISHMENT - A legal process to reach the money or effects of a defendant, in the possession or control of a third person.
GRAND JURY - Not less than 16, not more than 23 citizens of a county sworn to inquire into crimes committed or triable in the county.
GRANT - To agree to; convey, especially real property.
GRANTEE - The person to whom a grant is made.
GRANTOR - The person by whom a grant is made.
GRATUITOUS - Given without a return, compensation or consideration.
GRAVAMEN - The grievance complained of or the substantial cause of a criminal action.
GUARANTY (n.) - A promise to answer for the payment of some debt, or the performance of some duty, in case of the failure of another person, who, in the first instance, is liable for such payment or performance.
GUARDIAN - The person, committee, or other representative authorized by law to protect the person or estate or both of an incompetent (or of a *sui juris* person having a guardian) and to act for him in matters affecting his person or property or both. An incompetent is a person under disability imposed by law.
GUILTY - Establishment of the fact that one has committed a breach of conduct; especially, a violation of law.

H

HABEAS CORPUS - You have the body; the name given to a variety of writs, having for their object to bring a party before a court or judge for decision as to whether such person is being lawfully held prisoner.
HABENDUM - In conveyancing; it is the clause in a deed conveying land which defines the extent of ownership to be held by the grantee.
HEARING - A proceeding whereby the arguments of the interested parties are heared.
HEARSAY - A type of testimony given by a witness who relates, not what he knows personally, but what others have told hi, or what he has heard said by others.
HEARSAY RULE, THE - (a) "Hearsay evidence" is evidence of a statement that was made other than by a witness while testifying at the hearing and that is offered to prove the truth of the matter stated; (b) Except as provided by law, hearsay evidence is inadmissible; (c) This section shall be known and may be cited as the hearsay rule.
HEIR - Generally, one who inherits property, real or personal.
HOLDER OF THE PRIVILEGE - (a) The client when he has no guardian or conservator; (b) A guardian or conservator of the client when the client has a guardian or conservator; (c) The personal representative of the client if the client is dead; (d) A successor, assign, trustee in dissolution, or any similar representative of a firm, association, organization, partnership, business trust, corporation, or public entity that is no longer in existence.
HUNG JURY - One so divided that they can't agree on a verdict.
HUSBAND-WIFE PRIVILEGE - An accused in a criminal proceeding has a privilege to prevent his spouse from testifying against him.
HYPOTHECATE - To pledge a thing without delivering it to the pledgee.
HYPOTHESIS - A supposition, assumption, or toehry.

I

I.E. (id est) - That is.
IB., OR IBID.(ibidem) - In the same place; used to refer to a legal reference previously cited to avoid repeating the entire citation.
ILLICIT - Prohibited; unlawful.
ILLUSORY - Deceiving by false appearance.
IMMUNITY - Exemption.
IMPEACH - To accuse, to dispute.
IMPEDIMENTS - Disabilities, or hindrances.
IMPLEAD - To sue or prosecute by due course of law.
IMPUTED - Attributed or charged to.
IN LOCO PARENTIS - In place of parent, a guardian.
IN TOTO - In the whole; completely.
INCHOATE - Imperfect; unfinished.
INCOMMUNICADO - Denial of the right of a prisoner to communicate with friends or relatives.
INCOMPETENT - One who is incapable of caring for his own affairs because he is mentally deficient or undeveloped.
INCRIMINATION - A matter will incriminate a person if it constitutes, or forms an essential part of, or, taken in connection with other matters disclosed, is a basis for a reasonable inference of such a violation of the laws of this State as to subject him to liability to punishment therefor, unless he has become for any reason permanently immune from punishment for such violation.
INCUMBRANCE - Generally a claim, lien, charge or liability attached to and binding real property.

INDEMNIFY - To secure against loss or damage; also, to make reimbursement to one for a loss already incurred by him.
INDEMNITY - An agreement to reimburse another person in case of an anticipated loss falling upon him.
INDICIA - Signs; indications.
INDICTMENT - An accusation in writing found and presented by a grand jury charging that a person has committed a crime.
INDORSE - To write a name on the back of a legal paper or document, generally, a negotiable instrument
INDUCEMENT - Cause or reason why a thing is done or that which incites the person to do the act or commit a crime; the motive for the criminal act.
INFANT - In civil cases one under 21 years of age.
INFORMATION - A formal accusation of crime made by a prosecuting attorney.
INFRA - Below, under; this word occurring by itself in a publication refers the reader to a future part of the publication.
INGRESS - The act of going into.
INJUNCTION - A writ or order by the court requiring a person, generally, to do or to refrain from doing an act.
INSOLVENT - The condition of a person who is unable to pay his debts.
INSTRUCTION - A direction given by the judge to the jury concerning the law of the case.
INTERIM - In the meantime; time intervening.
INTERLOCUTORY - Temporary, not final; something intervening between the commencement and the end of a suit which decides some point or matter, but is not a final decision of the whole controversy.
INTERROGATORIES - A series of formal written questions used in the examination of a party or a witness usually prior to a trial.
INTESTATE - A person who dies without a will.
INURE - To result, to take effect.
IPSO FACTO - By the fact iself; by the mere fact.
ISSUE (n.) The disputed point or question in a case,

J

JEOPARDY - Danger, hazard, peril.
JOINDER - Joining; uniting with another person in some legal steps or proceeding.
JOINT - United; combined.
JUDGE - Member or members or representative or representatives of a court conducting a trial or hearing at which evidence is introduced.
JUDGMENT - The official decision of a court of justice.
JUDICIAL OR JUDICIARY - Relating to or connected with the administration of justice.
JURAT - The clause written at the foot of an affidavit, stating when, where and before whom such affidavit was sworn.
JURISDICTION - The authority to hear and determine controversies between parties.
JURISPRUDENCE - The philosophy of law.
JURY - A body of persons legally selected to inquire into any matter of fact, and to render their verdict according to the evidence.

L

LACHES - The failure to diligently assert a right, which results in a refusal to allow relief.

LANDLORD AND TENANT - A phrase used to denote the legal relation existing between the owner and occupant of real estate.
LARCENY - Stealing personal property belonging to another.
LATENT - Hidden; that which does not appear on the face of a thing.
LAW - Includes constitutional, statutory, and decisional law.
LAWYER-CLIENT PRIVILEGE - (1) A "client" is a person, public officer, or corporation, association, or other organization or entity, either public or private, who is rendered professional legal services by a lawyer, or who consults a lawyer with a view to obtaining professional legal services from him; (2) A "lawyer" is a person authorized, or reasonably believed by the client to be authorized, to practice law in any state or nation; (3) A "representative of the lawyer" is one employed to assist the lawyer in the rendition of professional legal services; (4) A communication is "confidential" if not intended to be disclosed to third persons other than those to whom disclosure is in furtherance of the rendition of professional legal services to the client or those reasonably necessary for the transmission of the communication.

General rule of privilege - A client has a privilege to refuse to disclose and to prevent any other person from disclosing confidential communications made for the purpose of facilitating the rendition of professional legal services to the client, (1) between himself or his representative and his lawyer or his lawyer's representative, or (2) between his lawyer and the lawyer's representative, or (3) by him or his lawyer to a lawyer representing another in a matter of common interest, or (4) between representatives of the client or between the client and a representative of the client, or (5) between lawyers representing the client.
LEADING QUESTION - Question that suggests to the witness the answer that the examining party desires.
LEASE - A contract by which one conveys real estate for a limited time usually for a specified rent; personal property also may be leased.
LEGISLATION - The act of enacting laws.
LEGITIMATE - Lawful.
LESSEE - One to whom a lease is given.
LESSOR - One who grants a lease
LEVY - A collecting or exacting by authority.
LIABLE - Responsible; bound or obligated in law or equity.
LIBEL (v.) - To defame or injure a person's reputation by a published writing.
(n.) - The initial pleading on the part of the plaintiff in an admiralty proceeding.
LIEN - A hold or claim which one person has upon the property of another as a security for some debt or charge.
LIQUIDATED - Fixed; settled.
LIS PENDENS - A pending civil or criminal action.
LITERAL - According to the language.
LITIGANT - A party to a lawsuit.
LITATION - A judicial controversy.
LOCUS - A place.
LOCUS DELICTI - Place of the crime.
LOCUS POENITENTIAE - The abandoning or giving up of one's intention to commit some crime before it is fully completed or abandoning a conspiracy before its purpose is accomplished.

M

MALFEASANCE - To do a wrongful act.
MALICE - The doing of a wrongful act Intentionally without just cause or excuse.

MANDAMUS - The name of a writ issued by a court to enforce the performance of some public duty.
MANDATORY (adj.) Containing a command.
MARITIME - Pertaining to the sea or to commerce thereon.
MARSHALING - Arranging or disposing of in order.
MAXIM - An established principle or proposition.
MINISTERIAL - That which involves obedience to instruction, but demands no special discretion, judgment or skill.
MISAPPROPRIATE - Dealing fraudulently with property entrusted to one.
MISDEMEANOR - A crime less than a felony and punishable by a fine or imprisonment for less than one year.
MISFEASANCE - Improper performance of a lawful act.
MISREPRESENTATION - An untrue representation of facts.
MITIGATE - To make or become less severe, harsh.
MITTIMUS - A warrant of commitment to prison.
MOOT (adj.) Unsettled, undecided, not necessary to be decided.
MORTGAGE - A conveyance of property upon condition, as security for the payment of a debt or the performance of a duty, and to become void upon payment or performance according to the stipulated terms.
MORTGAGEE - A person to whom property is mortgaged.
MORTGAGOR - One who gives a mortgage.
MOTION - In legal proceedings, a "motion" is an application, either written or oral, addressed to the court by a party to an action or a suit requesting the ruling of the court on a matter of law.
MUTUALITY - Reciprocation.

N

NEGLIGENCE - The failure to exercise that degree of care which an ordinarily prudent person would exercise under like circumstances.
NEGOTIABLE (instrument) - Any instrument obligating the payment of money which is transferable from one person to another by endorsement and delivery or by delivery only.
NEGOTIATE - To transact business; to transfer a negotiable instrument; to seek agreement for the amicable disposition of a controversy or case.
NOLLE PROSEQUI - A formal entry upon the record, by the plaintiff in a civil suit or the prosecuting officer in a criminal action, by which he declares that he "will no further prosecute" the case.
NOLO CONTENDERE - The name of a plea in a criminal action, having the same effect as a plea of guilty; but not constituting a direct admission of guilt.
NOMINAL - Not real or substantial.
NOMINAL DAMAGES - Award of a trifling sum where no substantial injury is proved to have been sustained.
NONFEASANCE - Neglect of duty.
NOVATION - The substitution of a new debt or obligation for an existing one.
NUNC PRO TUNC - A phrase applied to acts allowed to be done after the time when they should be done, with a retroactive effect.("Now for then.")

O

OATH - Oath includes affirmation or declaration under penalty of perjury.
OBITER DICTUM - Opinion expressed by a court on a matter not essentially involved in a case and hence not a decision; also called dicta, if plural.

OBJECT (v.) - To oppose as improper or illegal and referring the question of its propriety or legality to the court.
OBLIGATION - A legal duty, by which a person is bound to do or not to do a certain thing.
OBLIGEE - The person to whom an obligation is owed.
OBLIGOR - The person who is to perform the obligation.
OFFER (v.) - To present for acceptance or rejection.
    (n.) - A proposal to do a thing, usually a proposal to make a contract.
OFFICIAL INFORMATION - Information within the custody or control of a department or agency of the government the disclosure of which is shown to be contrary to the public interest.
OFFSET - A deduction.
ONUS PROBANDI - Burden of proof.
OPINION - The statement by a judge of the decision reached in a case, giving the law as applied to the case and giving reasons for the judgment; also a belief or view.
OPTION - The exercise of the power of choice; also a privilege existing in one person, for which he has paid money, which gives him the right to buy or sell real or personal property at a given price within a specified time.
ORDER - A rule or regulation; every direction of a court or judge made or entered in writing but not including a judgment.
ORDINANCE - Generally, a rule established by authority; also commonly used to designate the legislative acts of a municipal corporation.
ORIGINAL - Writing or recording itself or any counterpart intended to have the same effect by a person executing or issuing it. An "original" of a photograph includes the negative or any print therefrom. If data are stored in a computer or similar device, any printout or other output readable by sight, shown to reflect the data accurately, is an "original."
OVERT - Open, manifest.

P

PANEL - A group of jurors selected to serve during a term of the court.
PARENS PATRIAE - Sovereign power of a state to protect or be a guardian over children and incompetents.
PAROL - Oral or verbal.
PAROLE - To release one in prison before the expiration of his sentence, conditionally.
PARITY - Equality in purchasing power between the farmer and other segments of the economy.
PARTITION - A legal division of real or personal property between one or more owners.
PARTNERSHIP - An association of two or more persons to carry on as co-owners a business for profit.
PATENT (adj.) - Evident.
    (n.) - A grant of some privilege, property, or authority, made by the government or sovereign of a country to one or more individuals.
PECULATION - Stealing.
PECUNIARY - Monetary.
PENULTIMATE - Next to the last.
PER CURIAM - A phrase used in the report of a decision to distinguish an opinion of the whole court from an opinion written by any one judge.
PER SE - In itself; taken alone.
PERCEIVE - To acquire knowledge through one's senses.
PEREMPTORY - Imperative; absolute.
PERJURY - To lie or state falsely under oath.

PERPETUITY - Perpetual existence; also the quality or condition of an estate limited so that it will not take effect or vest within the period fixed by law.
PERSON - Includes a natural person, firm, association, organization, partnership, business trust, corporation, or public entity.
PERSONAL PROPERTY - Includes money, goods, chattels, things in action, and evidences of debt.
PERSONALTY - Short term for personal property.
PETITION - An application in writing for an order of the court, stating the circumstances upon which it is founded and requesting any order or other relief from a court.
PLAINTIFF - A person who brings a court action.
PLEA - A pleading in a suit or action.
PLEADINGS - Formal allegations made by the parties of their respective claims and defenses, for the judgment of the court.
PLEDGE - A deposit of personal property as a security for the performance of an act.
PLEDGEE - The party to whom goods are delivered in pledge.
PLEDGOR - The party delivering goods in pledge.
PLENARY - Full; complete.
POLICE POWER - Inherent power of the state or its political subdivisions to enact laws within constitutional limits to promote the general welfare of society or the community.
POLLING THE JURY - Call the names of persons on a jury and requiring each juror to declare what his verdict is before it is legally recorded.
POST MORTEM - After death.
POWER OF ATTORNEY - A writing authorizing one to act for another.
PRECEPT - An order, warrant, or writ issued to an officer or body of officers, commanding him or them to do some act within the scope of his or their powers.
PRELIMINARY FACT - Fact upon the existence or nonexistence of which depends the admissibility or inadmissibility of evidence. The phrase "the admissibility or inadmissibility of evidence" includes the qualification or disqualification of a person to be a witness and the existence or nonexistence of a privilege.
PREPONDERANCE - Outweighing.
PRESENTMENT - A report by a grand jury on something they have investigated on their own knowledge.
PRESUMPTION - An assumption of fact resulting from a rule of law which requires such fact to be assumed from another fact or group of facts found or otherwise established in the action.
PRIMA FACUE - At first sight.
PRIMA FACIE CASE - A case where the evidence is very patent against the defendant.
PRINCIPAL - The source of authority or rights; a person primarily liable as differentiated from "principle" as a primary or basic doctrine.
PRO AND CON - For and against.
PRO RATA - Proportionally.
PROBATE - Relating to proof, especially to the proof of wills.
PROBATIVE - Tending to prove.
PROCEDURE - In law, this term generally denotes rules which are established by the Federal, State, or local Governments regarding the types of pleading and courtroom practice which must be followed by the parties involved in a criminal or civil case.
PROCLAMATION - A public notice by an official of some order, intended action, or state of facts.

PROFFERED EVIDENCE - The admissibility or inadmissibility of which is dependent upon the existence or nonexistence of a preliminary fact.
PROMISSORY (NOTE) - A promise in writing to pay a specified sum at an expressed time, or on demand, or at sight, to a named person, or to his order, or bearer.
PROOF - The establishment by evidence of a requisite degree of belief concerning a fact in the mind of the trier of fact or the court.
PROPERTY - Includes both real and personal property.
PROPRIETARY (adj.) - Relating or pertaining to ownership; usually a single owner.
PROSECUTE - To carry on an action or other judicial proceeding; to proceed against a person criminally.
PROVISO - A limitation or condition in a legal instrument.
PROXIMATE - Immediate; nearest
PUBLIC EMPLOYEE - An officer, agent, or employee of a public entity.
PUBLIC ENTITY - Includes a national, state, county, city and county, city, district, public authority, public agency, or any other political subdivision or public corporation, whether foreign or domestic.
PUBLIC OFFICIAL - Includes an official of a political dubdivision of such state or territory and of a municipality.
PUNITIVE - Relating to punishment.

Q

QUASH - To make void.
QUASI - As if; as it were.
QUID PRO QUO - Something for something; the giving of one valuable thing for another.
QUITCLAIM (v.) - To release or relinquish claim or title to, especially in deeds to realty.
QUO WARRANTO - A legal procedure to test an official's right to a public office or the right to hold a franchise, or to hold an office in a domestic corporation.

R

RATIFY - To approve and sanction.
REAL PROPERTY - Includes lands, tenements, and hereditaments.
REALTY - A brief term for real property.
REBUT - To contradict; to refute, especially by evidence and arguments.
RECEIVER - A person who is appointed by the court to receive, and hold in trust property in litigation.
RECIDIVIST - Habitual criminal.
RECIPROCAL - Mutual.
RECOUPMENT - To keep back or get something which is due; also, it is the right of a defendant to have a deduction from the amount of the plaintiff's damages because the plaintiff has not fulfilled his part of the same contract.
RECROSS EXAMINATION - Examination of a witness by a cross-examiner subsequent to a redirect examination of the witness.
REDEEM - To release an estate or article from mortgage or pledge by paying the debt for which it stood as security.
REDIRECT EXAMINATION - Examination of a witness by the direct examiner subsequent to the cross-examination of the witness.
REFEREE - A person to whom a cause pending in a court is referred by the court, to take testimony, hear the parties, and report thereon to the court.

REFERENDUM - A method of submitting an important legislative or administrative matter to a direct vote of the people.
RELEVANT EVIDENCE - Evidence including evidence relevant to the credulity of a witness or hearsay declarant, having any tendency in reason to prove or disprove any disputed fact that is of consequence to the determination of the action.
REMAND - To send a case back to the lower court from which it came, for further proceedings.
REPLEVIN - An action to recover goods or chattels wrongfully taken or detained.
REPLY (REPLICATION) - Generally, a reply is what the plaintiff or other person who has instituted proceedings says in answer to the defendant's case.
RE JUDICATA - A thing judicially acted upon or decided.
RES ADJUDICATA - Doctrine that an issue or dispute litigated and determined in a case between the opposing parties is deemed permanently decided between these parties.
RESCIND (RECISSION) - To avoid or cancel a contract.
RESPONDENT - A defendant in a proceeding in chancery or admiralty; also, the person who contends against the appeal in a case.
RESTITUTION - In equity, it is the restoration of both parties to their original condition (when practicable), upon the rescission of a contract for fraud or similar cause.
RETROACTIVE (RETROSPECTIVE) - Looking back; effective as of a prior time.
REVERSED - A term used by appellate courts to indicate that the decision of the lower court in the case before it has been set aside.
REVOKE - To recall or cancel.
RIPARIAN (RIGHTS) - The rights of a person owning land containing or bordering on a water course or other body of water, such as lakes and rivers.

S

SALE - A contract whereby the ownership of property is transferred from one person to another for a sum of money or for any consideration.
SANCTION - A penalty or punishment provided as a means of enforcing obedience to a law; also, an authorization.
SATISFACTION - The discharge of an obligation by paying a party what is due to him; or what is awarded to him by the judgment of a court or otherwise.
SCIENTER - Knowingly; also, it is used in pleading to denote the defendant's guilty knowledge.
SCINTILLA - A spark; also the least particle.
SECRET OF STATE - Governmental secret relating to the national defense or the international relations of the United States.
SECURITY - Indemnification; the term is applied to an obligation, such as a mortgage or deed of trust, given by a debtor to insure the payment or performance of his debt, by furnishing the creditor with a resource to be used in case of the debtor's failure to fulfill the principal obligation.
SENTENCE - The judgment formally pronounced by the court or judge upon the defendant after his conviction in a criminal prosecution.
SET-OFF - A claim or demand which one party in an action credits against the claim of the opposing party.
SHALL and MAY - "Shall" is mandatory and "may" is permissive.
SITUS - Location.
SOVEREIGN - A person, body or state in which independent and supreme authority is vested.
STARE DECISIS - To follow decided cases.

STATE - "State" means this State, unless applied to the different parts of the United States. In the latter case, it includes any state, district, commonwealth, territory or insular possession of the United States, including the District of Columbia.
STATEMENT - (a) Oral or written verbal expression or (b) nonverbal conduct of a person intended by him as a substitute for oral or written verbal expression.
STATUTE - An act of the legislature. Includes a treaty.
STATUTE OF LIMITATION - A statute limiting the time to bring an action after the right of action has arisen.
STAY - To hold in abeyance an order of a court.
STIPULATION - Any agreement made by opposing attorneys regulating any matter incidental to the proceedings or trial.
SUBORDINATION (AGREEMENT) - An agreement making one's rights inferior to or of a lower rank than another's.
SUBORNATION - The crime of procuring a person to lie or to make false statements to a court.
SUBPOENA - A writ or order directed to a person, and requiring his attendance at a particular time and place to testify as a witness.
SUBPOENA DUCES TECUM - A subpoena used, not only for the purpose of compelling witnesses to attend in court, but also requiring them to bring with them books or documents which may be in their possession, and which may tend to elucidate the subject matter of the trial.
SUBROGATION - The substituting of one for another as a creditor, the new creditor succeeding to the former's rights.
SUBSIDY - A government grant to assist a private enterprise deemed advantageous to the public.
SUI GENERIS - Of the same kind.
SUIT - Any civil proceeding by a person or persons against another or others in a court of justice by which the plaintiff pursues the remedies afforded him by law.
SUMMONS - A notice to a defendant that an action against him has been commenced and requiring him to appear in court and answer the complaint.
SUPRA - Above; this word occurring by itself in a book refers the reader to a previous part of the book.
SURETY - A person who binds himself for the payment of a sum of money, or for the performance of something else, for another.
SURPLUSAGE - Extraneous or unnecessary matter.
SURVIVORSHIP - A term used when a person becomes entitled to property by reason of his having survived another person who had an interest in the property.
SUSPEND SENTENCE - Hold back a sentence pending good behavior of prisoner.
SYLLABUS - A note prefixed to a report, especially a case, giving a brief statement of the court's ruling on different issues of the case.

T

TALESMAN - Person summoned to fill a panel of jurors.
TENANT - One who holds or possesses lands by any kind of right or title; also, one who has the temporary use and occupation of real property owned by another person (landlord), the duration and terms of his tenancy being usually fixed by an instrument called "a lease."
TENDER - An offer of money; an expression of willingness to perform a contract according to its terms.
TERM - When used with reference to a court, it signifies the period of time during which the court holds a session, usually of several weeks or months duration.

TESTAMENTARY - Pertaining to a will or the administration of a will.
TESTATOR (male)
TESTATRIX (female) - One who makes or has made a testament or will.
TESTIFY (TESTIMONY) - To give evidence under oath as a witness.
TO WIT - That is to say; namely.
TORT - Wrong; injury to the person.
TRANSITORY - Passing from place to place.
TRESPASS - Entry into another's ground, illegally.
TRIAL - The examination of a cause, civil or criminal, before a judge who has jurisdiction over it, according to the laws of the land.
TRIER OF FACT - Includes (a) the jury and (b) the court when the court is trying an issue of fact other than one relating to the admissibility of evidence.
TRUST - A right of property, real or personal, held by one party for the benefit of another.
TRUSTEE - One who lawfully holds property in custody for the benefit of another.

U

UNAVAILABLE AS A WITNESS - The declarant is (1) Exempted or precluded on the ground of privilege from testifying concerning the matter to which his statement is relevant; (2) Disqualified from testifying to the matter; (3) Dead or unable to attend or to testify at the hearing because of then existing physical or mental illness or infirmity; (4) Absent from the hearing and the court is unable to compel his attendance by its process; or (5) Absent from the hearing and the proponent of his statement has exercised reasonable diligence but has been unable to procure his attendance by the court's process.
ULTRA VIRES - Acts beyond the scope and power of a corporation, association, etc.
UNILATERAL - One-sided; obligation upon, or act of one party.
USURY - Unlawful interest on a loan.

V

VACATE - To set aside; to move out.
VARIANCE - A discrepancy or disagreement between two instruments or two aspects of the same case, which by law should be consistent.
VENDEE - A purchaser or buyer.
VENDOR - The person who transfers property by sale, particularly real estate; the term "seller" is used more commonly for one who sells personal property.
VENIREMEN - Persons ordered to appear to serve on a jury or composing a panel of jurors.
VENUE - The place at which an action is tried, generally based on locality or judicial district in which an injury occurred or a material fact happened.
VERDICT - The formal decision or finding of a jury.
VERIFY - To confirm or substantiate by oath.
VEST - To accrue to.
VOID - Having no legal force or binding effect.
VOIR DIRE - Preliminary examination of a witness or a juror to test competence, interest, prejudice, etc.

W

WAIVE - To give up a right.
WAIVER - The intentional or voluntary relinquishment of a known right.
WARRANT (WARRANTY) (v.) - To promise that a certain fact or state of facts, in relation to the subject matter, is, or shall be, as it is represented to be.

WARRANT (n.) - A writ issued by a judge, or other competent authority, addressed to a sheriff, or other officer, requiring him to arrest the person therein named, and bring him before the judge or court to answer or be examined regarding the offense with which he is charged.

WRIT - An order or process issued in the name of the sovereign or in the name of a court or judicial officer, commanding the performance or nonperformance of some act.

WRITING - Handwriting, typewriting, printing, photostating, photographing and every other means of recording upon any tangible thing any form of communication or representation, including letters, words, pictures, sounds, or symbols, or combinations thereof.

WRITINGS AND RECORDINGS - Consists of letters, words, or numbers, or their equivalent, set down by handwriting, typewriting, printing, photostating, photographing, magnetic impulse, mechanical or electronic recording, or other form of data compilation.

Y

YEA AND NAY - Yes and no.

YELLOW DOG CONTRACT - A contract by which employer requires employee to sign an instrument promising as condition that he will not join a union during its continuance, and will be discharged if he does join.

Z

ZONING - The division of a city by legislative regulation into districts and the prescription and application in each district of regulations having to do with structural and architectural designs of buildings and of regulations prescribing use to which buildings within designated districts may be put.